ANGLESEY AND ITS
COASTAL TRADITION

Anglesey
and its Coastal Tradition

Mike Smylie

© Text: Mike Smylie

Copyright © by Gwasg Carreg Gwalch 2000.
All rights reserved. No part of thid publication may be reproduced
or transmitted, in any form or by any means, without permission.

ISBN: 0-86381-615-0

The author acknowledges the help of Menter Môn in the publication of this
book.

All illustrations by the author except those by Lewis Morris taken from his
1748 – Plans of Harbours, Bars, Bays and Roads in St. Georges Channel.
Thanks to Bridget and Graham Dempsey

Cover design: Siân Parry

First published in 2000 by
Gwasg Carreg Gwalch, 12 Iard yr Orsaf, Llanrwst, Wales LL26 0EH
✆ 01492 642031 📠 01492 641502
✆ books@carreg-gwalch.co.uk   Internet: www.carreg-gwalch.co.uk

For Mono, remembering those walks,
and that sail!

To see a world in a grain of sand
And heaven in a wild flower
Hold infinity in the palm of your hand
And eternity in an hour

William Blake 1757-1827

Contents

Introduction

During winters of 1997/98 and 98/99 I spent many hours pacing the coastal footpaths of Anglesey, my adopted home, as part of my on-going research into Britain's fishing boats and the folk who worked them. I walked past inaccessible beaches and rarely-visited coves, wobbled along narrow cliffpaths as the wind buffeted me, and wandered freely along great stretches of muddy shores with only the pebbles and seabirds to talk to. I spent hours listening to the different sounds the sea makes; to pebbles rattling as the waves recede and the howl of the wind as it makes itself both heard and felt. And yet, sadly, I hardly saw any signs of present day fishing. No boats lie on the beaches that fishermen once frequented in early morning chat. However, I purposely chose winter as the time of my incursions so that my thoughts wouldn't be diluted too much by the effects of tourism, upon which the economy of the island relies heavily. That's not to say I wasn't affected by it, only that I decided to lessen my discontentment.

One thing that soon became apparent was that I was going to be unable to write purely about the fishing, the one subject my previous books have covered. Anglesey, taken in a historical context, has always been well furnished with a fishery. It's shores welcome the sea, whether upon the gently-sloping beaches or the more reckless rocky coasts whose shape the sea has eroded and moulded over countless generations – generations no doubt that have survived from this shore as all coastal dwellers have done throughout man's evolution. Coastal communities were the egg of human organised society, and these themselves grew up out of the proximity of the sea and all its fruits. Today's fishermen, those that are left, are a fine body of men being slowly suffocated by government, and I'm saddened by their passing.

I wrote this book by concentrating upon the fishing, but not exclusively remaining in that domain. It is also about the general maritime life of the normal person living and working by the shoreline. I've tried to avoid too much repetition of what's been said before, although there's some, I guess, justification in saying that everything's been said somewhere before! But maybe not in one book.

Anglesey's coastline remains largely as unspoilt today as it ever has been, except in certain parts. Indeed much of this coastline has been classed, quite rightly, as an area of outstanding natural beauty. Although it is impossible to circumnavigate the island by only using its paths, large tracts of the coast are accessible to the intrepid walker. It is without doubt a fine coast to walk, with some of the most varied scenery to be found anywhere in the British Isles.

This book isn't intended as a walking guide – there are plenty of good ones that do that job. Neither are the maps intended to show the route. The Ordnance Survey maps do just that, and it is advised that both these items are obtained before venturing out. It is intended as a foretaste of what is to come and perhaps a small key to what once there was, and what can now be seen.

Chapter 1

Môn Mam Cymru

Out at the herring fishing

There are three ways to cross over from mainland Britain to the Isle of Anglesey. Most visitors use either Thomas Telford's suspension bridge or Robert Stevenson's Britannia bridge, the latter now having the original railway beneath the newer main A5 roadway. The third way is across the water by boat, the only way until Telford completed his crossing in 1826.

Anglesey is an island situated, for those without this knowledge, off the north coast of Wales, lying within the shadow of the beautiful Snowdonia, where tumbling rivers drop away from its mountain peaks and leafy valleys are dominated by its fearsome cliff faces. Like other coastal communities, Anglesey has largely depended upon the sea for its economic survival, although its fertile green fields have also contributed to its growth.

In the early eighteenth century one Daniel Defoe visited the island, crossing over from Caernarfon, moving along the west side to Holyhead and back through the centre to Beaumaris and across 'the Fretum, or strait of Meneu'. He was somewhat dismissal of the island, stating that 'there is nothing of note to be seen in the Isle of Anglesea, but the town, and castle of Beaumaris'. He continued by describing it as a very level and plain region, but with the land having earmarks of being fruitful and pleasant. Thus he notes ' . . . it is a much pleasanter country, than any other part of N. Wales, that we have seen; and particularly is very fruitful for corn and cattle'. Compare this Classical Period description with John Leland and his observations in the sixteenth century that 'there is a good commodite for fishinge about Tir Mon but their lacketh courage and diligence'. Another traveller suggested that Anglesey was 'naked and unpleasant', and not producing 10% of the possible yield. Yet it's name 'Môn, mam Cymru' (Môn, Mother of Wales) suggests, contrary to this, that it was readily able to, and in fact did at one time, supply the whole of Wales with grain. In 1770 alone more than ninety thousand bushels of grain – mostly barley and oats in preference to wheat – were produced from over fifty working windmills. No wonder it was regarded as the 'granary of Wales' until; that is, cheap imports of grain in the second half of the nineteenth century forced the farmers to turn to animal husbandry.

The early traveller, George Lyttleton, in his *An account of a Journey in Wales* was another one suggesting that the island didn't produce goods to its full potential. He reckoned that the population, though, were content with this state of affairs and that they were just happy to be self sufficient in their communal needs. These small communities contained all the necessary craftsfolk that were required for everyday life within them. People rarely moved from the area of their birth and trades were handed down through the family from father to son. It seems that this situation of community self sufficiency continued until the First Wold War when John Williams Brynsiencyn sent hordes of young men from the fields and shores of Ynys Môn to the killing fields of France and Flanders, and when outsiders first began to move onto the island in large numbers. Tourism over the next twenty years served to accentuate this modernising of island life. Whether the fishing developed to its full capacity, I guess, can never be fully determined as it seems impossible to calculate this capacity so many generations later. If farming was the mainstay of the economy, and the island was surrounded by stocks of herring for only a few months of the year, it follows that the farmers would leave the land in the autumn, at a time when the harvest had just been brought in, and with the land being left until the spring. They then took to the sea to try their hand at catching a small part of the shoals that served two notions – the first to feed the family on something

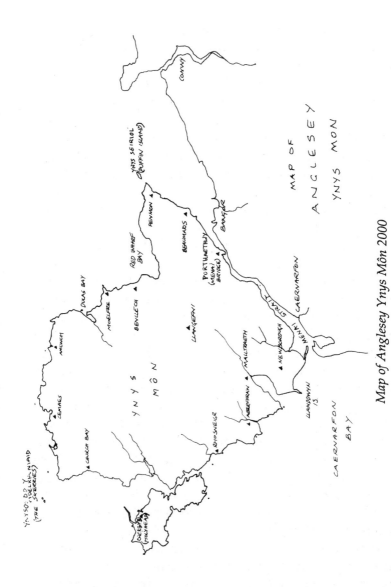

Map of Anglesey Ynys Môn 2000

YNYSOEDD Y MOELRHONIAID
(THE SKERRIES)

CHURCH BAY

CEMAES

AMLWCH

DULAS BAY

MOELFRE

RED WHARF BAY

BENLLECH

YNYS SEIRIOL
(PUFFIN ISLAND)

PENMON

BEAUMARIS

PORTHAETHWY
(MENAI BRIDGE)

LLANGEFNI

BANGOR

CONWY

MAP OF
ANGLESEY
YNYS MON

YNYS
MÔN

RHOSNEIGR

ABERFFRAW

MALLTRAETH

NEWBOROUGH

CAERNARFON

MENAI STRAIT

LLANDWYN IS.

CAERNARFON BAY

CAERGYBI
(HOLYHEAD)

14

different, and the second to bring in a not insubstantial income. It was a break from the monotony of bread, butter and salt beef, and a bit of money to supplement other desires.

In *The History of the Island of Anglesey*, Nicolas Owen (1775) notes that:

> 'since the failure of the herring fishery, with which these coasts were abundantly supplied, the potato has been much planted, and has made a principal part of the food of the inhabitants. Mr X says that because of their living on potatoes and not salted herrings as before, the number of inhabitants has increased on the island . . . the islanders frequently live to 80/90 years, are generally healthy and long-lived. The air of Anglesey is keen, but seldom tainted with infectious vapours'.

To a large extent, this remains the case.

However, in 1798, in direct contrast to Owen, Warner states that huge shoals of herring 'sometimes visit the Anglesea coast, which are taken, dried, and exported: being considered by the knowing ones in delicacies, as particularly excellent'. In actual fact, it was probably the case that herring did add to an otherwise tedious diet until the potato arrived to add further variation. And as the herring is notorious for disappearing altogether one year and returning equally suddenly another, a few years of scarcity might well lead to preference for the potato until the herring returned. At least with the potato they could rely upon a good yield, unless the blight attacked the crop.

Anglesey was, however, an inaccessible part of the

country. Caergybi (Holyhead) had been the terminal point for embarkation to Ireland since the days of Queen Elizabeth 1 and travellers thus had to put up with journeying through what was described in 1688 as some of 'the most heathenish country ever any man travelled'! Once the hardened traveller had reached the edge of the Menai Strait, he still had to get across it. This wasn't always just a simple ferry crossing.

Ferries have existed across the Strait since before the days of Edward 1's castle building at Beaumaris and Caernarfon. Indeed, stones to build Caernarfon Castle were transported across the water, according to surviving records. Some six ferries allowed sufficient choice depending on weather, time and intended itinerary, these being at Beaumaris, Garth, Porthaethwy, Min-y-don, Tal-y-foel and Abermenai. Most involved a short boat ride, although catching the Beaumaris Ferry necessitated a five mile journey across the dangerous and extremely inhospitable Traeth Lafan, where many a carriage became lost in bewildering surroundings and was eventually swamped by the incoming tide.

Returning to the subject at hand, herring fishing was perhaps more profitable once the country's infrastructure allowed cured herring to travel to markets. Telford's spectacular crossing at Porthaethwy in 1826 was a vast improvement on the ferries, but the arrival of the railway line to the island and the crossing of the Menai Strait by Stephenson's Britannia Bridge in 1850 created far more opportunity and the farmers and seamen were quick to see the benefits. More money could be made in the few weeks of the season than could be earned throughout the rest of the year. Only a fool would miss this opportunity.

Profitable fishing wasn't solely the domain of the herring. Oysters, mussels, cockles and lobsters also demanded a fair price at market, though, as we shall see, all manner of fish swam in the waters around the coast, until overfishing and pollution changed the nature of fishing in the twentieth century. This has turned what was once a way of life for coastal communities into an industry that has little chance of survival, except for the lucky few.

Lewis Morris was a pioneer of the eighteenth century and is truly one of the 'sons of Anglesey'. The eldest of four brothers, he was born in 1701 by the shores of Traeth Dulas, a sandy inlet on the north-eastern side of the island. Here, it has been said, he played naked upon the dark sands, and was fascinated by the always-present ships, and the seas that were their home. By 1724 he had become an estate surveyor on the Bodorgan Estate on the western side of the island. Here he first learned the art of mapmaking and no doubt were sown the first seeds of his desire to map out Anglesey. Before long, he was a customs official at Beaumaris, at which time he began his survey of the Welsh coast until he produced his *Plans in St Georges Channel – 1748*. Within this he published his *Observations relating to the Improvements that might be made in the Harbours whose plans are given: together with some Account of the Natural Commodities and Trade of those Places*. Indeed, this was an early account of the small harbours of Anglesey, and one to which I shall constantly refer as I relate the story of Anglesey's fishing in our journey around its coast. We'll visit its tiny coves and vast sandy beaches, its few harbours and inland seas, all of which add up to warrant the claim as an area of outstanding beauty. Throw in Snowdonia's backdrop, and its not surprising that people from all over the world come back time and time again to visit this jewel off North Wales's coast.

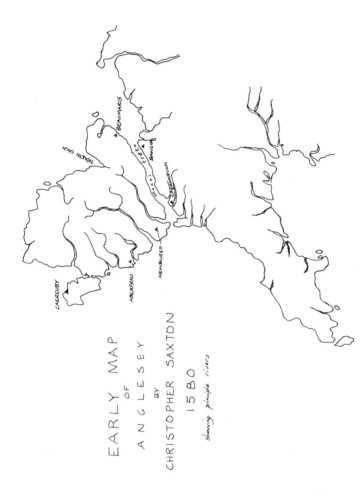

EARLY MAP
OF
ANGLESEY
BY
CHRISTOPHER SAXTON
1580
showing principle rivers

CAERGUBY
ABERFRAW
NEWBURGH
TRAETH LLOCH
BEAUMARIS
BANGOR
CAERNARVON

Early Map of Anglesey by Christopher Saxton 1580 showing principle rivers

19

Chapter 2

The Port of Beaumaris

Trwyn-du Lighthouse, Penmon

We begin our circumnavigation of Anglesey at the medieval centre of Anglesey's fishery. Here was the customs house where Lewis Morris once worked, and the fishery office that gives all the island's fishing boats their registration letters of BS. At least, that is, since the system of registration was introduced in the 1860s. Nowadays all signs of the trade are long gone, replaced, as in many other parts of the country, by hotels with high facades, day-trippers streaming in on coaches, yachts and yachtsmen's booming voices and fish-and-chip shops, beachware and tourist attractions. What else is there left for these redundant relics of industrial-age Britain? No wonder the people of Beaumaris complain to the council of excessive car parking fees. Driving away these tourists is like driving in the last peg of their destruction.

The town, with its very un-Welsh name, was born in the days of Edward 1. It was he who built the castle as part of his fortification of the entire Welsh coast. Started in 1296, it took some thirty years to almost complete. The name comes from *beau* and *mareys* meaning beautiful marsh, although Defoe refers to it as 'fine plain'. Marshland, it seems, reached from the very castle walls in all directions, and much of today's town has been built upon reclaimed land.

The castle itself was a superb example of early construction, although to many it was a sign of English repression of the Welsh. Built on the edge of the Strait, boats could come right alongside its walls to unload their cargo. The sea, over centuries, has regressed so that only a moat surrounds some of the castle. But, as a form of thanks, the king, fearful of the local population being too close for comfort to his stronghold, forcibly removed the inhabitants of nearby Llanfaes to Rhosyr in the south-west of the island, into a 'new borough' or Newborough (Niwbwrch) as it soon became.

Herring fishing was prosecuted in those days of castle building, and taxes were levied, no doubt to help with the costs of the project. In 1294, a tax of one penny per mease of herring was charged, and fishing boats entering and leaving the port were subjected to a further relinquishing of one mease of herring, worth at that time some two shillings. The tax raised amounted to about £60 each year – a not insignificant sum in those days! Whether this port tax included smaller fishing boats seems unclear, and probably unlikely, as a mease of herring equals 1240 fish, and would account for the whole catch on some days for these boats. What it does suggest is that larger fishing boats of substantial tonnage were fishing from the harbour, probably in deep water outside the Strait. However, it must be remembered that Beaumaris's jurisdiction covered the whole of the island, and parts of the mainland such as Bangor, so it is possible that not all the fish were actually landed in the town.

The Welsh Port Books furnish all researchers with a wealth of detail of the period between 1550 and 1603. They show that salt was imported from the Cheshire mines via Chester. Salt herring was exported back to both Chester and Liverpool. The Books suggest a boom in the fishery in the late sixteenth century, about the time John Leland was writing of a good commodity in fishing. A century later the Corporation of Beaumaris Minute Book (1694-1723) notes two packers of Fish as being employed by the town in 1722 and 1723. Richard Morris and Lewis Davies, presumably, oversaw the packing of the fish, checking the quality of the product and making sure the barrels were properly filled and sealed. That they only begun their jobs in 1722 suggests good years for fishing, although it is unknown for how long they remained thus employed.

Sir John Brampton observed in 1631 while crossing

the Strait that 'we did see some fisherboats'. Richard Bulkeley of Beaumaris 'sent a ship or two to Greenland for cod, ling and other fish, with which he bartered in Spain for sherry wine'. During this period Britain was sending hundreds of ships across to Greenland and Newfoundland, the majority from the West Country, in search of the huge shoals of cod being reported. The sea was said to have been so full of cod that the fishermen could lean over and take them with a hand net!

Thomas Pennant, the renowned eighteenth century writer from near Mostyn, wrote of Beaumaris that

'there is a very good anchorage for ships in the bay which lies before the town: and has seven fathom of water even at the lowest ebb. Vessels often find security here in hard gales. The town has no trade of any kind, yet its custom house for the casual reception of goods'.

The export of herring was obviously in severe decline.

Lewis Morris, in his 1748 Plans of Harbours, Bars, Bays and Roads in St George's Channel, supports this. He describes the town thus:

'Beaumaris was a Place of good Trade formerly, and might be so still, if the Inhabitants pursued it, it being an excellent Harbour, well situated, and well supplied with the Gifts of Nature'.

He also noted a thriving herring fishery and that

'this coast abounds with oysters: those of Penmon was fat and large, and famous for pickling. They have Muscles (sic), Cockles and other Kind of Fish, in Pleanty'.

What other kind of fish he doesn't elaborate, but, in 1770, it was written that the natural fish of the island were: 'Cod, Salmon, Herring, Thornback, Ling, Ray, Haddock, Plaice, Whiting, Seatrout, Turbot, Soles, Flounders, likewise Oysters, Crabs, Lobsters, Shrimps, Prawns, Mussels and Cockles in abundance'.

Shrimps were caught off the town. Indeed all along the North Wales coast the shrimp enjoyed the flat sandy beaches, as they did in Morecambe Bay, to the north. In the nineteenth century it was customary for the local nobbies – smack-rigged boats originating in Morecambe Bay, but which were later built in Conwy and Hoylake – to trawl for shrimps to supply an everlasting desire for the tasty crustaceans in the developing holiday resorts such as Rhyl, Colwyn Bay, Llandudno and Beaumaris. Morecambe, Southport and Blackpool had similar fleets. The Victorian trippers came to the coast from the Lancashire cotton mills in their droves as the railway opened up the coast to them, and Victorian shrimp teas – shrimps, bread and cup of tea – became a firm favourite. The shrimps were cooked in boilers aboard the nobbies as they loose their freshness quickly to become an inedible mush, so that they could be bought direct off the fishermen when they landed. And, as the railway that brought the holiday-makers in developed, so did the export of fresh fish to the distant markets of Liverpool and Manchester. Fishing rapidly turned from a level of subsistence to a booming industry. With this came the need of centralisation and the decline in small coastal fishing communities. Link this with the development of steam and motorisation, the increase in the size of trawls, the resultant over-fishing and the influence of bankers, and we see the beginnings of a declivity that is all too apparent these days.

George Borrow perhaps realised some of this in 1862 when he reported Beaumaris as second to none as a watering place. 'Steamers brought Victorian visitors from Liverpool and Llandudno.' It wasn't just the railway but the building of steam ships that facilitated the spread of tourism.

Herring nets continued to be set in nearby Fryar's Bay into the twentieth century. Small rowing boats were utilised for the task. Several nobbies worked from the town up to at least 1939, one being the *Lettice*, a 35ft nobby. Another boat, *Joyce*, a 25ft ex-naval cutter, modified by having a half-deck built over the fore part, trawled for some of the year, taking trippers out to Puffin Island in the summer. This boat had a four cylinder Kelvin petrol/paraffin engine in her, and petrol cost 1/4d a gallon before the last war. Fishermen were able to reclaim the tax element back on this. One more boat, an East coast smack, was owned by Sir George Witchcot, who often returned with a healthy catch which he then sold around the town from a barrel. However, like nearly all of the fishing activity in the town in the twentieth century, it was summer-seasonal. Only occasional jaunts to the winter herring was the exception..

One reminder of the days of medieval fishing around Beaumaris are the record of a pair of fish-traps on the beach in front of the town. Fish-traps were common-place throughout Wales, and have been in existence since very early times. Indeed, Neolithic man stopped the mouths of rivers and narrow tidal creeks and used barbed stone hooks to catch the stranded fish. Fish was probably first caught in this way after being found in natural rockpools until man realised he could improve his luck by building similar, but larger, barriers. The Scots caught herring in very early times in their *yairs* (Scots) or *cairidh* (Gaelic), and nets later on became a natural progression from these fixed weirs.

In 1438 the *lyme-kiln* weir stretched across part of the shore known as *lyme-culne*, as far as the *feryman warth*, and was leased for 20 years to Thomas Norrey. Ten years later a second weir becomes apparent 'lying between the *lyme-kylne* fishery and the house of the Friar Minor of Llanfaes'. The rent paid by the fisherman, Thomas Sherwin, was sixpence a year. However, pin-pointing the position of these weirs proved impossible on a recent visit. Another weir, lying off Gallows Point, was leased for only four pence a year between 1451 and 1491. A recent hunt proved this to be elusive as well.

Gallows Point has a tradition of ship and boat building stretching back a long time. Although the site was formerly where prisoners from Beaumaris gaol were hanged, Beaumaris ships sailed the oceans in the eighteenth and nineteenth centuries, loaded with Welsh slate and copper. Nowadays, although some boatbuilding still continues, the main source of income is from repairs and winter storage. Presently, plans are afoot to build a marina; a development, although unwelcome to many, which will probably benefit some

P. 3.

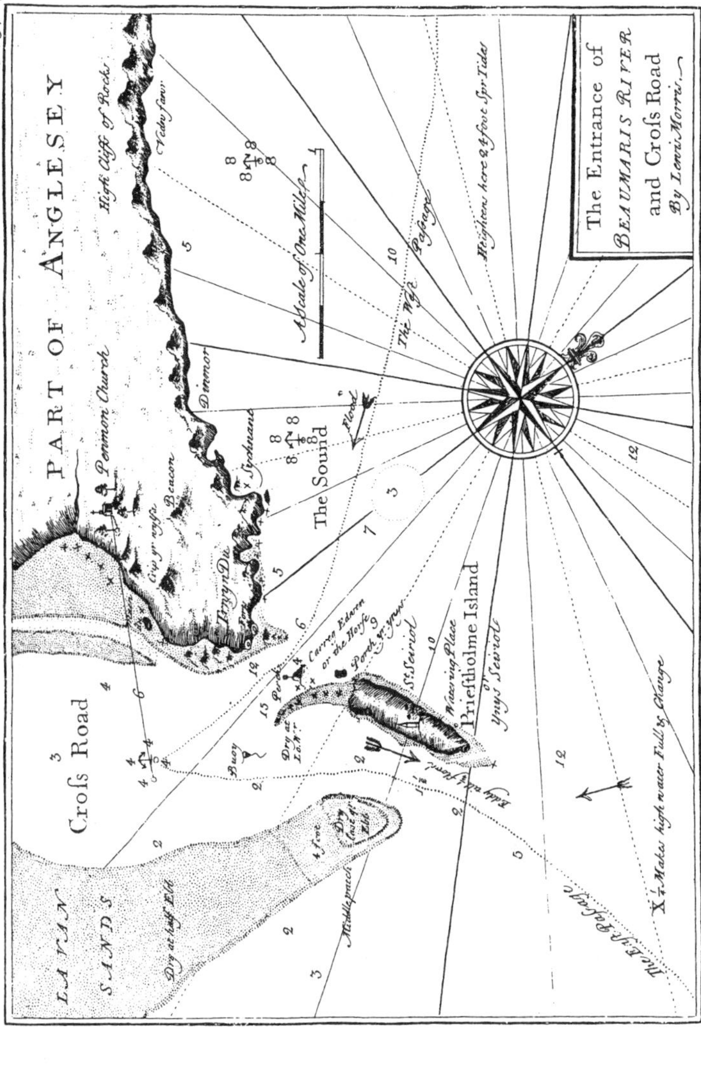

Nach. Hill Sculp.

Publish'd According to Act of Parliament Sep.t 29. 1748

in the town. Yachts, though, once played an important part in the town. One renowned, although now dead, boatbuilder's great-grandfather was an Essex oyster-fisherman, who came to the island in search of the shellfish with his smack. In the summer the grandfather worked on the racing yachts, those smart-looking boats that were part of the gentlemanly way of life in the mid-eighteenth century. During the sailing season, the fishermen often crewed aboard, learning as much about boat handling as they received in wages. This occurred all over Britain, in the Clyde, the Solent, the Essex backwaters and on the Thames in the main, wherever the rich Victorian masters brought their expensive, and fast, yachts.

A couple of miles east of the town lies the remains of the old lifeboat station, which can be reached easily on foot. Here a lifeboat house with its deepwater roller slipway had been built in 1914 to replace the lifeboat stationed along the coast at Penmon, until its closure in 1991 and subsequent dismantling. Directly alongside the few signs of the steel ramp lay the remains of a fish weir that was in operation until the 1960s. Called the *gorad bach* (little weir), the trap had last been worked by two brothers, John and Wilf Girling. It consisted of stone walls, about four feet high and up to eight feet wide, into which stout oak posts had been driven. Some of the boulders in the walls were massive. Hazel, or sometimes willow, was interweaved about the posts, some of which still remain today. For the first two feet above the walls, the weave was very dense, while the top five feet was more open to allow the water to flow through freely when the current was at its strongest. The wall followed a line, parallel to the lifeboat house, that went directly from the top of the beach straight to the water's edge, and then followed a line at right-angles, parallel and level to the low water mark, perhaps a few feet above it at spring tide. Then, at the right-hand end, the wall followed a sharp angle back on itself, forming a trap, or crew as it was called, into which the fish were eventually forced as the tide ebbed. At high tide the fish would swim over and around the back of the weir, only then to become trapped as the tide fell and they couldn't escape in the direction of the ebb.

This weir had been in constant daily use until its abandonment by the two brothers. In fact the lease had belonged to the family ever since their grandfather had come up from Devon in the 1860s. It seems he originally came to grow oysters along the beach until the lease was offered a few years later. Throughout their ownership the family had made a living from its operation, living in the house directly above at the top of the beach, where their daughter still lives today. They caught mackerel, herring and whitebait, bass and salmon, and sometimes all manner of weird fish, including the strange, green-boned, garfish. Along the bottom part of the wall was a bass trap which was a gateway with a grating set into it. When opened before the tide had completed ebbed, any whitebait could escape, quickly to be devoured by the ravenous bass and salmon that tended to linger outside. These were then netted using lap-nets fixed onto poles. The same nets were used to capture the fish in the weir at low tide, when they would be thrashing around in the shallow water in the crew of the weir.

The upkeep of such a structure was immense. Any gale usually inflicted some damage, and local willow was cut to repair the weave. Spruce was often used to replace the oak posts. Stones from the beach mended any breach in the walls. But after all this work, on some days there were no fish in the trap when the tide had fallen. Yet on others boxes of herring and whitebait would be carried laboriously up the beach. Like any other type of fishing, the fishermen were at the mercy of the elements and fate!

The Girlings sold their fish locally in their own fish shop, and they supplemented their catch by trawling with their small nobby *Siren*, which had a model T Ford engine. However, in the 1960s, with visitors and locals alike often deciding that the fish in the trap was theirs for the taking, and with a decline in the fortunes of fishing on the Strait, the Girlings eventually abandoned their weir, and the sea and bait-diggers both helped it to crumble. However, talking to a fellow recently, he told me how he remembers well the two brothers taking five hundredweight of whitebait from the trap on one occasion. Mackerel, he mused, sold for a tanner each at the same time.

Another mile eastwards along the beach, a bigger weir was once in operation. This, the Trecastell weir, was worked until the 1920s, and was supposedly much more effective, it being over twice as big as the *gorad bach*. However, it followed the same shape, with its crew pointing in the direction of the flood tide.

Castell Aberlleiniog sits upon a mound by a small stream that flows onto the beach by this larger weir. Half-hidden now by trees, this castle was built of wooden walls in 1090, only to be destroyed a few years later, then rebuilt in stone, and being finally pulled apart in 1646. However the intriguing point is that, according to early maps, this stream was in fact quite a wide inlet which may have allowed ships to sail right up to the castle walls to unload their wares. Today the stream is only a few feet wide and perhaps a foot deep, but, assuming the same regression of the sea that is measurable at Beaumaris, it is entirely plausible that fishing boats once worked here. The castle, at the time of its construction, would have been situated at a particularly good vantage point with a command of boats on the Strait, over two hundred years before Edward I was building his chain of fortifications.

Moving east once more, again along both the beach and the road, we come to Penmon on the eastern tip of the island. Lewis Morris referred to the harbour here from where great quantities of millstones were shipped from the nearby quarries. In 1775 it was reported that 'Penmon has a good harbour and plenty of oysters, remarkably large: the poor find constant employ in the dredge, and in pickling the fish for foreign consumption'. Today the Dinmor quarries remain as gigantic amphitheatres gouged out of the bare rock. Some buildings remain littered around the site, now quiet, as if standing as a testament to the sweat and graft of previous generations. A small quay, built in the nineteenth century for this export of stone, still remains.

Trwyn Du lies half a mile to the east, and is the actual most easterly tip of Anglesey. This point has to be reached along the road as the quarries prevent access along the coast. Be warned though, when driving a vehicle along this road. On a recent trip to photograph the lighthouse, I was accosted by a nasty man who demanded £1.50 for driving the few hundred yards along the road. Although there is a sign stating that it is a toll road, there is no mention of such a high fee. When I refused to pay on the grounds that this amounted to a car parking fee and I wasn't stopping, he began to punch my vehicle and threatened to pull the wing mirror off! Beware the little man who has not a local accent!

Here a black and white painted lighthouse guards the narrow Sound between Anglesey and Puffin island, and has done so since it was built in 1831. In that same year the *Rothesay Castle*, a passenger steamer, was driven ashore here in gale-force winds, killing all but twenty of the one hundred and fifty people on board. Puffin Island, so called because of the nesting birds, stands perhaps four cables offshore. It was called Ynys Lenach in the twelfth century, when the island was deemed out-of-bounds for all women. The Vikings called it Priestholm, and the Welsh call it Ynys Seiriol, after the saintly hermit who established a monastery there in the sixth century.

Pennant reported that 'puffins appear in April, displacing rabbits from their burrows who flee to the other side of the island. Puffins lay one egg and feed off sprats and seaweed. Young puffins are pickled and preserved in spices'. These, it seems, were caught and pickled in barrels about twelve inches long and fetched between three and four shillings apiece.

Of fishing hereabouts, Pennant mentions 'three new species taken in the channel between Priestholm and Anglesey – Beaumaris shark, Morris and Trifurcated Hake. The first appears to be a sort of porbeagle shark, whilst the second, a small larval stage of a conger eel, was first reported in 1793 by William Morris, brother of Lewis, hence its name. Four were caught off Beaumaris about the beginning of the nineteenth century, one in the Trecastell fish weir, which was reported to be about three miles distant from Beaumaris, and the other three below the Beaumaris green whilst prawning amongst the seaweed at low water.

Penmon still has its old coastguard cottages, although they are privately owned now. The nearby lifeboat house, too, has been converted into a dwelling. The lifeboat was first stationed here in 1831, until being transferred to nearby Moelfre in 1848. The present boat-house was built in 1880, and was operational until the lifeboat was moved to the new Beaumaris station in 1914.

Between Penmon and Traeth Coch (Red Wharf Bay) the coast is wild and inaccessible, and was once described as follows: 'the shore is very rude, and terrific to navigators, and many of its rocks fine and picturesque, rising to a great height'. The only fishing hereabout is offshore, or more often within the realms of the rod and line brigade who line the rocks when the weather is suitably calm. These people reach the coast on foot, but specialised knowledge is critical to prevent accidents on the rocks.

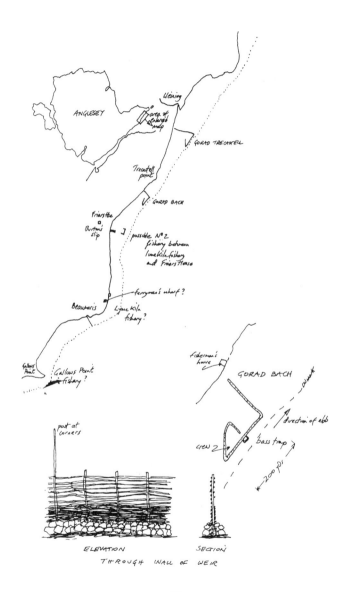

ANGLESEY

Lleiniog

area of enlarged scale

GORAD TREOATELL

Treoatell point

V GORAD BACH

Friarsthe

Burton's slip

possible Nº 2 fishery between lime kiln fishery and Friars House

ferryman's wharf?

Beaumaris

Lyme kiln fishery?

Gallows Point

Gallows Point fishery?

Fisherman's house

GORAD BACH

current

direction of ebb

crew

bass trap

200 yds.

post at corners

ELEVATION
THROUGH WALL OF WEIR

SECTION

35

Chapter 3

The Beach ran Red with Blood

Point Lynas lighthouse '99

Traeth Coch (Red Wharf Bay), according to Lewis Morris, was a hive of activity in the eighteenth century. Thus he wrote that

> this place lying open to the North Westerly winds, makes it necessary to have a small pier, which might be made under Porthllongdy, for about Two Hundred Pounds; there being plenty of Stones at hand, and all other materials.

He must surely have been referring to the north-westerly wind that blows in over the low ground of the island, as the bay faces east. Although perhaps not as frequent as westerly winds, it must be easterly winds that would be of more concern to boats working from the beach here. If anything, the part of the bay under Porthllongdy actually affords most shelter from north-westerly winds, although the Irish Sea is fickle and uncomfortable swells can run in around many headlands.

Over the next two hundred years plans for the development of the bay were suggested on two further occasions. The first of these was in 1812, when a scheme to build a railway for the carriage of coal from the Pentre Berw mines to Porthllongdy was devised, along with the construction of a quay to simplify the loading of the coal boats. Nothing was ever made of this plan, although the drawings still survive. However, in a report prepared by the County Council for the North Wales Development Council in 1947, a proposal for the building of a small pier was again put forth. Still no pier was built and the bay remains exposed from the east, although a nib of shingle does afford some degree of shelter. Today sailing and small pleasure-fishing boats lie on the sand at low water, and only at high water are they at risk from the wind. Personally I wouldn't be upset if the whole lot were wrecked in a storm, so indifferent these craft are in comparison to the graceful ships of the past. Characterless objects, and I include boats, are generally a reflection of our present attitude to a consumer society in which individualness is suppressed for the sake of mass-production.

Morris describes the natural marine life of the bay thus:

In this Bay there are Herrings in plenty, and other

Kind of Fish, of which the Inhabitants here make great Profit.

Indeed, in his plan of the wide, expansive bay, he notes a weir at the extreme southern edge of the bay under the mound of Bwrdd Arthur (Arthur's Table). I can find no sign of this fish weir remaining today, save that it is still clearly marked on the Ordnance Survey map of the area. Herring most certainly favoured the sandy seabed in autumn.

Stone from the quarry at Castell Mawr, the large, square-shaped mound that is the most dominant feature of the edge of the bay, was used to build both Caernarfon and Beaumaris castles, and was later taken to Liverpool for the construction of the harbour and many other city buildings. The other so-called commodities were limestone, the marble that Morris suggested 'would make Columns for Public Buildings' and the sand that was rich and perfect for use as manure. He reported that sloops transported this sand to 'all parts of Anglesey', and supposedly this manure yielded greater crops of oats and barley than other manure could.

The Vikings came here to invade the coastal-dwelling Welsh. One battle that ensued was a particularly bloody one, and the blood of both sides ran on top of the sand, turning the whole bay a bright red. Hence the local name of the bay, Traeth Coch (red beach).

Shipbuilding at Porthllongdy developed in the eighteenth century without Lewis Morris's suggested pier. All the protected estuaries of Wales saw some degree of shipbuilding in the late eighteenth and early nineteenth centuries as the quarries and mines expanded. The 81 ton sloop Eleanor was built here in 1786. She spent most of her working life carrying copper ore from Amlwch to Liverpool. Between 1766 and 1840 some eight ships were built upon the sands here.

One last proof that this site has remained a place of trade for centuries is the amount of port dues paid by visiting craft. Records go back to 1407 when, it is said, a sum of 16s 8d was received, a princely amount at the time.

Coastal footpaths are a great way to discover coastlines. In many cases these follow ancient paths which coastal dwellers used for access to other parts before the days of the motor car. Today they have been largely reopened, and hundreds of miles of British coasts can be visited in this way. Anglesey is extremely well endowed with such rights of way and they are particularly beneficial for coastal research. Traeth Coch is a suitable place to begin a walk as the path from Beaumaris is largely inaccessible.

It's only a short walk around Castell Mawr, along the sandy beach to Benllech. The village now sprawls up the hill away from the beach, a seething mass of bungalows and caravans and a popular watering place in the summer season. That the village centre lies up the hill suggests that it did not originate as a fishing village. Quarrying at one time produced exceptionally fine quality black and grey marble that was loaded into ships directly off the beach. Being sandy and flat, it was perfect for this purpose, and the same perfection now persuade the holiday-makers to frequent it in the season. For the same reason, the fishermen from the village of Moelfre, to the north, also often landed their catch here, in preference to their own beach. The reason was two-fold – the first being that the herring was often taken directly offshore from here and the second, more importantly perhaps, being that the all-important railhead was at Benllech.

In 1908 the railway was brought into the village from Pentre Berw, on the main Holyhead LNR route, but taken no further. Although, as a passenger line, it was short lived – passengers were only carried until 1930 – it did survive longer, until 1950, as a freight line. This enabled fresh fish to be quickly taken from Benllech to the markets of Chester, Manchester, Liverpool and Birmingham. One old fellow told me recently how he remembers the specially chartered fish train that everyday took the local fish off to these distant markets.

Today the track has been dismantled and the bridges left to fall apart. Cattle, sheep and wildlife are the only dwellers on the embankments and in the shelters below the remains of these bridges. However the route is clearly identifiable and follows a route relatively close to the suggested plans of 1812, along the valley of Afon Ceint and through nearby Pentraeth. The old wooden station building itself is derelict, hidden amongst trees, but the old station house survives as a private house.

Benllech did have one or two fishermen with their own boats. One disadvantage of using the beach to off-load the catch was the distance up it at low water. Often the herring was put into sacks and carried up the beach on their backs, and the boats were left until the tide flooded. Sometimes a local farmer or merchant with a horse and cart could be persuaded, with some fish as bait, to haul the sacks up to the railhead. At other times they were taken up the hill by pushcart, a tedious burden at any time, and even more so after a hard night's fishing. Eventually, though, the age of the motor vehicle brought in lorries, making this delivery job much easier.

Now take the path at the northern end of the beach, past the cafe, and you find yourself meandering between high hedges, with caravans on one side and the rocks the other. Excellent views over Benllech sands towards Ynys Seiriol and the Great Orme (y Gogarth) are the reward. Past lonely Borth Wen and onwards along the clifftop, below which the wave platforms shine as the sparkling sea washes over them. Sometimes the path seems to overhang the cliff, supported as it is by wooden logs driven in and wedged with pegs. Through bracken and fern, and then trees that envelope the path, until suddenly the path emerges over Traeth Bychan. Down past the ruin of a lovely old traditional Welsh cottage. I always wonder why these buildings are passed over in favour of the ugly ones that the council allows to be put up. It is one of those rural enigmas that aesthetic buildings are either ripped down or simply left because they aren't deemed suitable for our present needs. One thing that wrecks many parts of the countryside, and Anglesey is

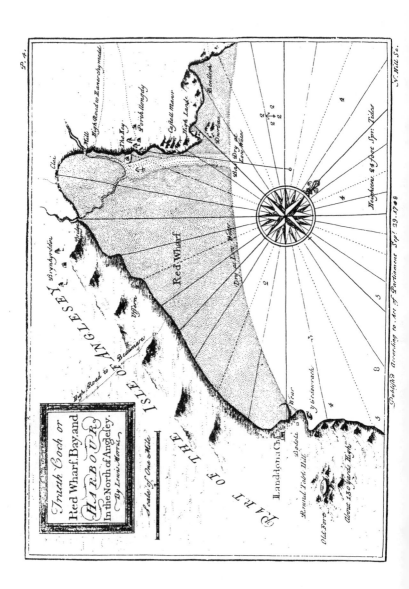

Traeth Coch or
Red Wharf Bay, and
HARBOVR,
In the North of Angelesey.
By Lewis Morris.

Scale of One Mile.

no exception, is the design of some of these latterday monstrosities which are just so out of keeping with tradition. It is a great pity especially as this coast is, in places, a perfect example of the lack of honest planning control.

On the morning that I visited this peaceful scene, the quietness was abruptly destroyed by two of those confounded jet-skis starting up their monotonous engines. I watched them as they buzzed around, like unwanted flies, in ever-decreasing circles. I am forever astonished that people actually get enjoyment from what appears to be a pretty dumb pastime as they destroy the calm of their surroundings. And why do they always have to dress in such abysmally coloured wetsuits? Even the machines, with their incessant howling, come in shades of yellow, red and green that surely should be reserved the artist's canvas!

Nestling into the northern end of the beach is the little harbour once described as being perfectly 'positioned for sloops to load and unload away from the swell'. The harbour, although the entrance still consists of two stone piers some thirty yards apart, appears to have been formed at the back of the cliff itself. Although tidal it is easy to imagine very large sailing boats mooring up here to load millstones from the nearby quarry. It seems that the quality of the millstones quarried hereabout were unsurpassed, and they were exported all over Britain including, in 1314, one purchased for the sizeable sum of 28/9d by the Royal Mill in Dublin. Doubtlessly many of the fifty windmills of Anglesey that helped contribute to its becoming called the granary of Wales had stones that came from this quarry. Today, though the harbour is home to an odd collection of pleasure boats, it remains an idyllic spot.

Rejoining the coastal path in the field above the tiny harbour, it's a short walk over to the small pebbly beach at Porth yr Aber where an iron winch, which was surely used for hauling up boats, still faces the sea. Following the path above the rocks brings the walker out at Moelfre.

Whereas Beaumaris was once the centre of the herring export trade, Moelfre was the centre of the actual fishing. Moelfre herring were renowned all over the island, and many folk still recall the times when the cry of 'Moelfre herring' heralded the arrival of the fishermen's wives hawking their fish. Moelfre men were amongst some of the finest seamen Wales has produced, and they sailed the seven oceans upon trading vessels delivering goods to every corner of the world. They often only came home for the herring season which began in October and continued through till February. To join them came men from Amlwch, Porth Llechog (Bull Bay), Cemlyn and Cemaes.

The open boats they used were 16ft (4.8m) long, clinker-built boats, many of which were built by Matthew Owen of Porthaethwy (Menai Bridge). Others were built by the fishermen themselves, although this was rarer than in many other parts of Britain. Prior to the season the boats were prepared by being scraped, scrubbed and re-painted. White paint was used above the water-line and inside and coal tar was brushed on below the water-line.

These boats were used to take the nets out to the intended fishing grounds. Sometimes these were set just offshore of Moelfre, and at other times taken the three miles to the Benllech shores. A single lugsail was set in the latter case, but the boats were simply rowed with two oars if they were staying close to their home shore. The nets themselves were fixed nets – i.e. they were anchored to the sea bed and not used as drift-nets. The nets were about 30 feet (9m) long and 10 feet (3m) in depth, and a normal train had eight nets attached to form a continuous wall of netting some 240 feet (73m) long. In the early herring season the nets had twelve meshes to the foot and this was reduced in dimension to thirteen meshes per foot as the fish decreased in size after they had spawned. The nets were taken out each Monday morning and laid out with stones at each end as anchors. They were then hauled up each morning with the fish being removed before being set once more. They were hauled in and taken ashore each Saturday, so that no fishing was practised on a Sunday. However, if gales blew up during the week and the fishermen weren't able to get out, it was often the case that the nets would get all twisted and tangled up, so that they had to be lifted as soon as the weather abated, allowing the men to get to sea. The tangled mess of nets were taken to a field to be sorted and repaired, often by the womenfolk of the village. The nets in general seldom survived much longer than four or five weeks of work, and they were never barked in preservative to help them last longer.

The benefit of the money earned from the herring was felt throughout the village. When high wages were received – sometimes two or three months of fishing could realise twice as much as the average annual earnings – the money was spent around the shops and pubs. The young fishermen never thought twice about buying a new suit from the tailor for £5. Likewise the baker and butcher benefitted. The pubs, although the women of the village frowned upon the antics of the drinkers within them, did a roaring business. It was said that the pub by the beach did more business before 6 am than it did throughout the rest of the day during the herring season. Often, when dealing with the fish buyer who bought the majority of the catch, the bartering of the price took place inside the pub. These barrels were then loaded onto a horse and cart and carried to the railhead at Benllech. Some of the herrings were smoked locally.

The herring fishery in Moelfre didn't really continue past the outbreak of war in 1939. The boats, with names such as Sovereign, Seagull, Stag or Shamrock, were left idle on the beach, only occasionally being taken out to lift the few lobster pots that were set offshore. The beach fell quiet until the holiday-maker found this most tranquil of villages and put it on the tourist map of Anglesey. Today, though, it remains largely undeveloped and unspoilt so that its placidity has survived.

The coastal footpath continues north, past the lifeboat house which was built in 1909 – the previous lifeboat was at Porth Neugwl and was first stationed there in 1875 – and around past Ynys Moelfre. A few hundred yards further and the memorial stone to the

Royal Charter can be seen just above the path. The wreck of the ship lies buried in the sand below the rocks. This iron sailing ship of 2719 tons, which also had an auxiliary 200hp motor, was driven ashore in hurricane conditions in 1859. Four hundred and fifity-nine people were drowned and half a million pounds worth of gold bullion from Australia lost to the beach. Although much has been salvaged, there is still a vast quantity lying beneath the seabed.

There's a story about Will and Jinnie Jones who lived close by at that time. Out picking winkles together off the beach, Will chanced upon a handful of gold sovereigns lying under some seaweed, presumably from the wreck, and showed them to Jinnie. Unbeknown to them, the wily village butcher-cum-coastwatcher Dan was spying on them and taking gold off the beach was illegal. So Jinnie went home with the booty while Will continued to pick winkles. When Dan arrived to confront the poor fisherman, Will denied having any knowledge of gold coins. Dan, of course, didn't believe him for one moment as he was sure he'd seen him find something that shone. So he hastened after the retreating Jinnie, with Will close on his heels. Luckily Jinnie arrived home first with a bit of time to spare, before Dan arrived, followed by Will. Dan insisted on searching the house, as was his duty, while Jinnie set about to stew the gastropods for dinner. Eventually, on being unable to find any incriminating evidence, Dan admitted that he must have been wrong. Being indifferent to Dan and his zest, the two invited him to stay and share their meagre meal of periwinkles, and he readily accepted. The three of them sat down and ate, with the coastguard leaving quite soon afterwards. Will could hardly contain his excitement, although he couldn't work out where the gold was. 'Wher've you hidden them, then,' he cried, only for Jinnie to look at him and declare them close at hand. 'Heb fod ymhell,' she said – 'not very far away'. 'Oh, Will bach,' Jinnie said after a few more minutes of watching his confusion, 'they've been lying at the bottom of the stew pan under the winkles all the time.' They both laughed so loudly, they were afraid that Dan would hear them and come back to see what it was all about.

Porth Forllwyd is the next beach afterwards. A tiny quay was built here in the nineteenth century, from which stone was loaded onto small trading sloops that plied between Dublin, Liverpool and Anglesey. More recently it serves as a bit of shelter for a solitary fisherman who works his lobster pots close to the shore. The sand by the quay dries out completely at low water.

Passing the beautiful sands of Porth Llugwy, (both Lewis Morris and the Ordnance Survey maps note an old fish weir here) which teems with visitors in the summer, the path arrives at Bae Dulas. These were the sands that Lewis Morris played upon as a boy, his family home overlooking the bay. Dulas, according to Morris, was home to a thriving herring fishery in his time. It was also the centre of a flourishing shipbuilding industry in the eighteenth century. The bay has a narrow entrance, perhaps only yards across at low water, and it is perfectly sheltered from winds from

Herring fishermen at Moelfre early 20th centuary
(photo: Anglesey County Record Office)

The beach and coast at Moelfre. The little white house to the left
of the pub could easily have been Huw Fish's house.
(photo: Anglesey County Record Office)

The beach at Moelfre with fishermen discussing the morning's catch
(photo: Author's collection)

Moelfre beach with a collection of fishing boats on the beach
(phoyo: Author's collection)

The harbour at Amlwch about the turn of the century
(photo: Author's collection)

A very old nineteenth century print of the harbour at Cemaes Bay at low water
(photo: Author's collection)

Cemaes with fishing boats in the foreground

The treacherous north coast of Anglesey – along the coastal footpath, 1998.
(photo: Author's collection)

*Along the coastal footpath – the old brickworks at Porthwen
stand out amongst the autumnal colours
(photo: Author's collection)*

*Porth Wen – looking east – with Amlwch in the background – 1998
(photo: Author's collection)*

53

The tiny harbour at Traeth Bychan. The boats are: top left – Sarah of Beaumaris built Chester 1832 wrecked 1911: bottom left – Darling of Beaumaris built 1781 wrecked 1893: right – a Mersey steam flat quarried stone was exported, mainly to Liverpool, but also further afield. Photo must predate 1893
(photo: Anglesey County Record Office)

Typical double–ended fishing boat – the Janet, BS87, at Porth Llongdy, Red Wharf Bay.
(photo: Anglesey County Record Office)

Another view of the previous photo. The Sloop BS13 is probably a welsh Nobby – similar to the shrimping nobbies of Lancashire.
(photo: Anglesey County Record Office)

Beaumaris pier and the snow–clad mountains
(photo:Author's collection)

The small stone quay at Penmon where stone was exported from the quarries in the background
(photo: Author's collection)

Puffin Island and the lighthouse at Trwyn Du, this short crossing can be treacherous at times!
(photo: Author's collection)

The old lifeboat house at Penmon which was closed in 1915. It is now a private house.
(photo: Author's collection)

The beach at Rhosneigr with a lobster fisherman and his boat c.1900
(photo: Anglesesy County Record Office)

Rhosneigr's lifeboat – the 'Thomas Lingham' in 1918
(photo: Author's collection)

A typical Anglesey cottage – Llangwyfan church is in the background
(photo: Author's collection)

Twilight over a wintery Aberffraw – 1998
(photo: Author's collection)

The line of the fish trap at the mouth of the River Alaw in autumnal colours
(photo: Author's collection)

The breech at the western end of the trap where water was allowed out but the fish to stay in. Now the tide pours out on the ebb.
(photo: Author's collection)

Pilots Cove, Llanddwyn, at the launching of the lifeboat in 1906. First opened in 1826 and closed ten years later, it was re–opened in 1840 until being finally abandonned in 1907. The lifeboat house, as do the pilots' cottages, still remain.
(photo: Author's collection)

Mat–making in Newborough c.1900
(photo: Author's collection

Telford's picturesque Menai SuspensionBridge over the trees of Coed Môr
(photo: Author's collection)

The southern fish trap of Ynys Gorad Coch is just visible to the right of the island, as is the tower of the curing house over the other buildings
(photo: Author's collection)

Three generations of fishermen from 'Whitebait Island' (Ynys Gorad Goch)
left to right Madog Jones: Madog Jones: Madog Willie Jones
(photo: Anglesey County Record Office)

The remains (1999) of the 'Gorad Ddu' weir from the railway bridge
(photo: Author's collection)

Owen Matthew's boat–building shed at Ynys Faelog, Menai Bridge in 1997.
(photo: Author's collection)

The remains of the fish trap at Ynys Castell, Cadnant River, Menai Bridge in 1998.
(photo: Author's collection)

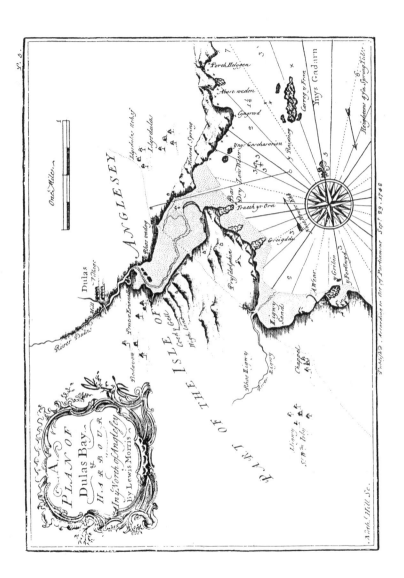

A PLAN OF
Dulas Bay
HARBOUR
In ye North of Anglesey
by Lewis Morris

ANGLESEY

One Mile.

Dulas
River Dulas
Hill
Tidse
Gadairn
Llygadwst ? Uchys
Llyadulas
Finiat Spring
Abert. weden
Porch Holwden
Gangrwd
Ynys Carchardron
y Rawing
Carreg y Fran
Imys Gadairn
Bay Low Water
Dry
Traeth yr Ora
Greigddy
Abert
Gorllun
yr Portlach
Ligary
Sands
Ankeriad Dibb
Boulacon
Pwer Francos
High Land
Coed y Gell
ISLE OF THE

Prydylphin
Pilot Ligary
Kiver Ligary
Ligary
Chapel

PART OF THE

A. Toms del Hill Sc.

Publish'd According to Act of Parliament Sep.r 29. 1748.

Heighwns of ye Spring Tides

nearly every direction. Offshore lies Ynys Dulas, where a beacon was built in 1824 to warn shipping of the danger. The tower also has a shelter for shipwrecked sailors, and was at one time kept stocked with food and water. Northwards from Dulas Bay the coast is generally inaccessible until the north-eastern tip of the island is reached at Trwyn Eilian or Point Lynas.

Chapter 4

Copper and Fish Seldom Mix!

Skerries lighthouse '99

Trwyn Eilian (Point Lynas) is a long finger of land jutting into the sea, and has been a threat to shipping in and out of Liverpool Bay for over three hundred years. Indeed the old Welsh name for the headland was Trwynybalog (the Jutting Point). The first beacon was built in the late eighteenth century when a pilot station was first established here in 1781. The present day lighthouse, dating from 1835, was erected by the Trustees of the Liverpool Docks. The Liverpool pilot boats were stationed here, kept afloat on moorings in the shelter of Porth Eilian. An easy walk from the beach, past the slipway on the east side of Trwyn Eilian that allowed access on this side when the weather was suitable, brings one to the grand lighthouse. The slipway today is a modern structure, of timber, steel and concrete, but its aspect certainly evokes a feeling of vulnerability when a strong east wind blows! The light of the lighthouse is interesting, being a semicircular glass window with a static light, not revolving, that juts out from the square tower like a bay window.

The pilot boats that once worked from here were six-oared vessels in the eighteenth century, until larger cutters were adopted in the following century. These were, unusually, schooner-rigged vessels, of which there were twelve up to 1896, all owned by the Mersey Dock Board after 1881. Before then they were owned by the pilots themselves and, prior to legislation in 1769, they were controlled by pilots who often either overcharged for their services, or simply didn't venture out if they felt to the contrary. The three-masted sprit-rigged watermen's gigs from Liverpool harbour, that regularly searched for incoming ships so as to be first to attend to their needs, were often anchored here as well, while awaiting further work.

Returning to Porth Eilian along the grassy path, with fine views along the north coast of the island, one is struck by the beauty of the area. Trees kiss the rocky water's edge and the hillside climbs up amongst farmhouses and gorsy fields. However caravans now intrude upon the peace of the hill over to the east, where they share their place with the tiny church of St Eilian. The beach itself is home to a few boats that are moored in the lee of the rocks, but these are wholly pleasure craft. Holiday-makers and divers use the beach in the summer, but throughout the rest of the year it is quiet.

A two-mile walk in a westward direction along the cliff path that skims the precipitous edge, through gorse, brings one to Porth Amlwch. This was once described as 'one of the most important ports in Wales'; yet it was only a natural creek in the mid-eighteenth century, occasionally frequented by local fishing boats, and was deemed to be unsuitable for visiting craft. In 1775, although still a small cove, the tiny harbour was recorded as being forty perches long and five perches wide. When the tide was in, 'it was nothing strange to see men fishing while they stand only at the brim of the cavation: in this agreeable pastime they avoid those commotions often concomitants of sea-fishing. The pilot boats were stationed here until being moved to Porth Eilian in 1781.'

Today Porth Amlwch is full of boats, and most of these are again pleasure craft. However several fishing boats do work from the harbour. The extent of the work that was done to increase the size of the port is visible, although it is but a shadow of its heyday when copper was being exported from here. For it was copper, from the mines on nearby Mynydd Parys, that accounted for the expansion during the second half of the eighteenth century. Copper had been mined here since the Roman days but, once a second mine was opened in 1775, the amount of ore being extracted jumped in quantity, necessitating greatly increased loading facilities. Ten years later the mines were supplying the navies of Holland, France and Spain, as well as Britain, with all their needs. Sheathing and copper nails were the most important uses for the metal, but it came to be used in other ways, especially in alloys. Then, in 1793, an Act of Parliament entitled 'An Act for enlargening, deepening, cleansing, improving and regulating the Harbour of Amlwch in the Isle of Anglesey' was passed. Ships from all over Britain, some of which were built on Anglesey, took the ore away, much of this going to the smelters of South Wales.

Between 1786 and 1825 some 29 ships were built in Anglesey, but only one of these was built at Amlwch. Shipbuilding, it appears, was not a tradition at the port.

By the time the nineteenth century dawned, some twenty smelters were working in the town as production from the mines grew to 44,000 tons a year. Trade exploded, and in 1825 James Treweek opened a shipbuilding yard and launched his first boat – the 68 ton sloop *Unity*. More boats followed in subsequent years, including the 130 ton brigantine *James and Jane* – the largest wooden boat ever built at the port – in 1830. Treweek's sons later joined him in his venture and one of them, Nicholas, opened a yard at Hirael, Bangor in 1842, but only one boat appears to have been built there – the 74 ton schooner *Mary*.

The Treweeks built the 160 ton *Mary Catherine* at Amlwch in 1859, the first iron ship to be constructed in Wales. That same year they moved into new premises, nearby, with the old yard being sold to William Cox Paynter who, although he concentrated more on ship-repairing, continued building in his own right until his death in 1881. Captain Thomas Morgan continued after him, again focusing on ship-repairing; yet he, too, built three more vessels between 1884 and 1898. Old Treweek died a few years after moving, and his sons took over with Nicholas, it seems, in control.

Captain William Thomas, who sailed many of the Treweek-owned ships, bought out Nicholas Treweek's new shipbuilding enterprise, with its carpenter's shop, smithy, counting house and sail loft in 1872. It is possible that Thomas already owned a yard in Amlwch as, after the take-over, he ran an advert in the local paper announcing the deal in which 'yards' is mentioned, as is also another yard in Duddon, Cumberland which came with the buy-out.

Thomas died in 1893 and the business passed to his sons Lewis and William. These two produced some of 'the finest vessels built of their time'. The port itself, with dry docks that enabled three ships to be built side by side, peaked in about 1890, and afterwards slipped into severe decline from which it never recovered, largely because of a slump in the fortunes of the mines due to foreign imports. However W. Thomas & Sons continued building up to 1908, when their last sailing vessel, the *Eilian*, was launched. Four years later the hospital ship *Morfudd* was launched and the war years yielded four ammunition barges, but by the end of hostilities work had finally ceased ending a tradition of over a century of shipbuilding. Between 1825 and 1918 seventy new vessels were launched at the port.

Another two miles west, along a footpath that circumvents the chemical works before joining the main road, is the hamlet of Porth Llechog with its east-facing beach. Although now a popular tourist spot, fishing played an important part in the community up to the last century. As has already been mentioned, several of the fishermen with their open, clinker-built boats, joined the Moelfre herring fishery during the season. At other times, especially during the summer, lobster fishing was the mainstay fishing activity, when the locals weren't either working on the land or away at sea. The pots were set within a few hundred yards of the cliff, yet difficulties were experienced because of the strong tides which can reach up to 5 knots at spring tides. According to an investigation into the Lobster Fishery of Wales for the Ministry of Agriculture, Fisheries and Food (A.C. Simpson 1955), this part of the Welsh coast, between Llandudno and Rhosneigr was the least fished for lobsters in the entire rocky coastline of Wales. A lifeboat was stationed at Porth Llechog in 1868, and this remained in service until 1926, saving sixty-three lives during that period.

It's possible now to rejoin the coastal footpath for a five mile walk to Cemaes. This follows the coast for two miles, winding through green fields, around headlands, through heather and over rock. The relentless sea moves back and forth some fifty feet or more below the clifftop, and it is easy to imagine how treacherous fishing would be in such tidal conditions. Before long the semi-circular bay of Porth Wen appears around a headland. Here, on the western edge of the bay, are the remains of the remote brickworks of the same name. Three bee-hive kilns stand by the quayside, with the incline from the quarry at Craig Wen above still clearly discernable. Bits of machinery litter the site, and buildings lie partially collapsed. The whole place is a bit eerie in its delapidated state, appearing as if the workforce had just up and left, and the works having

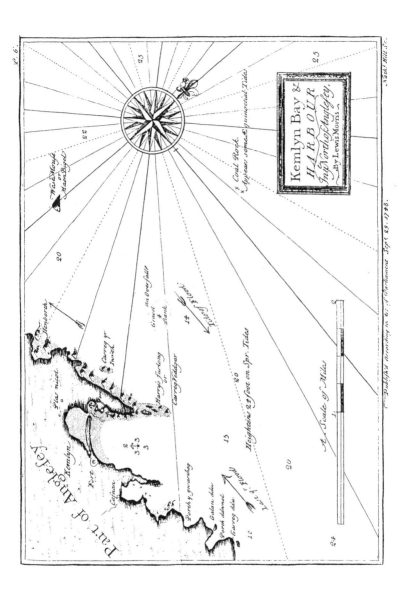

Kemlyn Bay &
HARBOUR
In ye North of Anglesey,
~ By Lewis Morris ~

+ Coral Rock
+ Appears some & provincial Tide

Wales Wolfe
or
Maen Bugel

A Scale of Miles

Par.t of Anglesey

Henborth

Pta: uchaf

Carreg y
Twrch

Harrys Jurdon
or
Carreg Padzur

Graig an Overfall
+
Plank

1st Flood

Port.

Cafnau

Porch y gwarbog

Golan dale

Porch islanod

Carreg dale

Height.d 2½ foot on Spr. Tides

2nd Flood

2
3 ⟶ 3
3

10   15   20

Publish'd according to Act of Parliament Sep.r 29. 1748.

Nath: Hill Sc.

p. 6.

been completely ignored since. Which is probably the case!

Continuing west the path winds to the lookout on Dinas Gynfor, Wales's most northerly point; beyond, it leads to Llanlleiana, and its associated ancient port from where the locally dug china clay was exported. Further on is the fifth century church of St Padrig, and beyond the village of Cemaes.

The present harbour wall of Cemaes was re-built in 1935 after the previous one was reputedly destroyed in a gale sometime before 1828. Even before this, the fishermen of Cemaes were said to have been salting herring. Again, considering the strong tides off the north coast of Anglesey, caused in the main by the rough nature of the seabed, presumably most of this herring was netted off the east coast of the island, and brought back to the village by boat. Much more recently plaice has been caught using trammel-nets in the bays during the summer season. Cod and whiting has been caught in the summer using hand-lines off the Skerries, the islands to the west, which will be described later.

The harbour was developed through the export of stone while importing coal and limestone for local use. Ships were built here in the nineteenth century when one Ismael Jones was producing vessels of between 100 and 400 tons. He is reputed to have employed sixty people in his yard, although records only account for three ships that he launched between 1825 and 1840. If he did employ such a large workforce, one must surmise that he built more ships than these three to survive. The port declined with the arrival of the railways to nearby Holyhead and Amlwch, enabling goods to be brought in to the area by rail.

The Cemaes lifeboat was established in 1872 at Porth Ogof, a mile or so to the north-west of the village, in a deep water and well sheltered cove. This was stationed in a wooden building upon a ramp, the stumps of which can still be seen on the beach. The island just offshore was utilised to support the ramp. The station closed in 1932, after saving thirty-two lives in its sixty years of existence and attending sixty vessels, one for each year of operation.

The massive bulk of Wylfa Nuclear Power Station lies to the west of Cemaes, the village lying in the shadow of this unknown entity. Although the site does create employment for many within the area, it's ugly facade always seems to threaten, mainly because of the havoc and destruction it is always capable of causing. Perhaps its outfall pipes haven't contributed much to the coastal fisheries either, considering the small number of fish found these days in the area. Mind you, with three or four nuclear plants around the Irish Sea, it's surprising that any normal, healthy fish are caught in this sea!

Cemlyn Bay, a mile further west, is a pebbly beach with a lagoon behind it, which is a nature reserve maintained by the North Wales Wildlife Trust. Fishing about Cemlyn has only been a summer pastime, when plaice were caught in the bays, and cod and whiting by hand-line. However, as we've seen, these fishermen came from Cemaes. Lobsters and crabs were in abundance during the summer, as they tend to move into deeper water in winter. In 1922, Owen H. Parry of Glanaber, Penrhyn, wrote in a letter of 1921 that the herring fishermen were 'doing quite well here being on a very small scale'. Again this referred to the Cemaes men. Lewis Morris makes no mention of Cemlyn in his account.

Cemlyn is the home of the first lifeboat on Anglesey. In the three years from 1825, some twenty or more ships were wrecked on the north coast of Anglesey. Although people tried to assist those who were in peril, they were largely unable to do so because of the nature of the coastline. Canon Owen Lloyd Williams, the rector of Llanfair-yng-Nghornwy, and his wife Frances, formed the Anglesey Lifesaving Association after they had witnessed one particular nasty shipwreck near Cemlyn. This was the ship *Alert* that sank with the loss of one hundred and forty-five lives. They vigorously raised funds to buy a lifeboat and the first one, a 32ft (10m) open boat, arrived in Cemlyn in 1828, having been designed by the M.P. and merchant George Palmer of Nazing Park, Essex, who was renowned as being a most efficient designer of these boats. It remained on station until 1919.

Hen Borth is a tiny bay facing north-west that had one 13ft (4m) lobster rowing-boat working from the beach in 1954 crewed by two men. These fishermen set approximately twenty pots during the summer. The beach lies empty today.

The Skerries (Ynysoedd y Moelrhoniaid) are a group of islands lying about two miles north-west of Trwyn-y-Gader (Carmel Head), the headland that marks the north-west tip of Anglesey and which lies two miles along the coastal footpath to the west of Hen Borth. Rising over the islets is a lighthouse which has heeded ships to the danger of these outlying reefs for over two hundred and fifty years. The first lighthouse was built by an Irishman, William Trench in 1716, and in 1725, at his death, tenure passed to his widow's son-in-law, his own son having been drowned while delivering coal to the island for the beacon. Five years later an Act of Parliament allowed the collecting of dues from each passing vessel which in effect became light dues. This amounted to one penny per ton for each British vessel except ships of war, and twice that for foreign ships. The visibility of that first light was said to be 7 or 8 leagues, an impressive distance given that one league was approximately three miles. The island remained under the family control until Trinity House took over the responsibility for the light in 1841 after purchasing the island, this being the last lighthouse in the country to come under their jurisdiction.

However, before this, the Skerries and the outlying islands belonged to the Bishop of Bangor who reported plenty of fish in the vicinity in the fourteenth century. Whitings and pollocks were taken all year round while, during the summer, blackfish – or colefish – were still taken by the basket by the lightmen and passing fishermen centuries later. Seals were caught in the fourteenth and fifteenth centuries, three instances being recorded of men being accused of poaching and being aquitted at court. Lewis Morris also reported 'Sea-Tench, Whiting-Pollacks and other Fish' being taken by rod from the rocks.

The view from Carmel Head is staggering, affording views over to Holyhead and its mountain, right along the northern coast of Anglesey and sometimes over to the Isle of Man. Offshore is the little Maen y Bugail (West Mouse) with a white-painted beacon. On shore stand the two White Ladies, two bigger beacons that align with the one on Maen y Bugail, and which were built to help shipping negotiate Carmel Head.

Just beyond is a chimney above the remains of a copper mine dating from the eighteenth century. It is said that there is evidence hereabout of mining in prehistoric times.

Continue over the headland, past Penbrynyreglwys, where there was once a church and, supposedly, a Roman lookout to guard Holyhead harbour, and the path drops down to Ynys y Fydlyn. Once the sea came right inland here and perhaps had been a fine place to beach a small boat. But today the area is quiet, and the only sign of humanity is the rubbish on the beach! The path continues over the headland, over a part where access is only allowed from 1 February to 14 September, and then through what is termed a permissive path – this doesn't appear to be a public right of way – and eventually to Porth Swtan (Church Bay).

Swtan is the Welsh for whiting which suggests that large quantities of the fish were landed here. Naming a cove after the fish the men most often brought ashore was common throughout these coastal communities. However, although there's a stone slipway leading steeply down to the beach, it's doubtful that any whiting is landed here now. Lobsters are the delicacy in the local Lobster Pot restaurant, although many of these are brought onto the island. However, it's a delightful setting and the lobsters are excellent.

The coast southwards can be followed in the main along the coastal footpath. It is a mixture of rock and sandy beaches, some of which might have made perfect landings for beach-based craft. However there doesn't seem to be any details of anyone fishing this part of the coast until the mouth of Afon Alaw is reached. Shipbuilding flourished here in the eighteenth century, but of more interest, perhaps, is the stone fish weir that lies across the river mouth, nearly completely blocking the seawater in its continual flood and ebb between Beddmanarch Bay and the river.

The stone wall of the weir is some four feet (1.2m) thick, and made up of fair-sized rocks. It's height has been reduced by both the action of the sea and mankind to between three and five feet (1-1.6m) high, and runs some 300 yards (270m) along the line of the river, slightly diagonally across, before running another 100 yards (90m) at an angle of about 150 degrees to the first run, pointing inshore. There's a twenty foot gap between the end of the weir and the opposite bank at low water. This gap enabled the water to escape on the ebb and the fish to swim upriver on the flood. During the ebb, the fish were pushed into the weir due to the tendency of the current to veer southwards, thereby trapping them. Although the weir now consists of low stone walls, extra height would have been built up using oak posts and willow weave, in the same way as the Beaumaris traps were built. Once the tide had receded, the fish would have been removed from the trap using lap-nets. It is said that this fish trap is ancient, but there seems to be no confirmation of this. Still, it is well preserved, and gives a good insight into these structures.

We now leave this part of the coast as we cross over the Stanley Embankment, the northerly boundary of the enclosed tidal channel between Anglesey and Holy Island, locally called the Inland Sea.

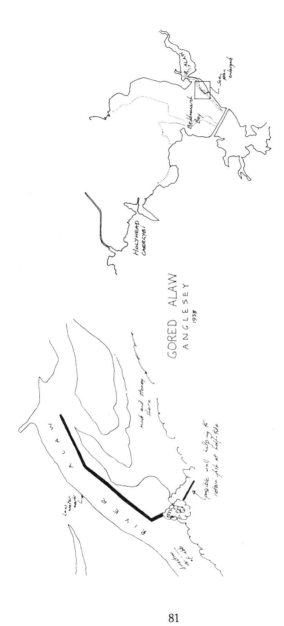

Gored Alaw Anglesey

Chapter 5

Beyond the Inland Sea

South Stack lighthouse '99

Crossing the three-quarters of a mile (1.2km) over the southern part of Beddmanarch Bay, and named after the family of the liberal MP for Anglesey between the years 1837-74, William Stanley, the embankment was the final obstacle on the long and arduous route from Shrewsbury to Caergybi (Holyhead). Completed in 1822, it was opened four years before Telford's Menai Suspension Bridge. In the days before the embankment there was a crossing over the sands to the north of here. The only other possible crossing was by making a detour to Rhyd-bont (Fourmile Bridge) where a bridge predated 1675. The first noticeable thing after crossing the embankment is the toll-gate house that was built to collect the tolls on the London to Holyhead main road, after Telford had successfully completed the route.

We leave the roadway here, and follow the path through the Penrhos Nature Reserve, alongside Beddmanarch Bay. This leads round to Gorsedd-y-penrhyn and eventually to Traeth Penrhos. Although the path isn't necessarily a public right of way, the route is possible, but anyone using it should check first.

The Romans built a stronghold at Caergybi in the fourth century which might have been rebuilt by Cadwallon Law Hir a hundred years later. The following century St Cybi arrived to build a monastery here which survived until the thirteenth century, although Vikings attacked it during the latter century of the first millenium. St Cybi used to meet St Seiriol from Penmon at Llannerch–y–medd every week, so it is said, and because St Seiriol always walked with his face away from the sun, he became Seiriol Wyn (the white one) while St Cybi was the lucky one, always walking towards the sun and so becoming Cybi Felyn (the tanned one).

However it was it's position as an excellent port for the crossing over to Ireland that enabled the small hamlet to grow. During the seventeenth century troops were taken over to Ireland from here, and it seems that the authorities kept a tight rein on all passing through the port because of espionage and gathering of intelligence Passports were needed and checked, and the vigilant troops were always suspicious of any abnormal movement. Not greatly different from today, I guess!

The packet service dates backs to the seventeenth

century, and possibly before, although records are sparse. By the mid part of the century there seemed to be two options for the traveller wishing to get to Ireland. Either he took the erratic boat from Chester, or journeyed along the North Wales coast through what was described as some of the 'most heathenish country man ever travelled' by one itinerant writer in 1688. Not until the final link in the railway – Stevenson's Britannia Bridge across the Menai Strait – was completed in 1850, could the journey from London to Holyhead be made without stoppages. Letters between Ireland and Holyhead took about six days and cost eight pennies to send.

When Lewis Morris worked here in the middle of the eighteenth century there were three packet-boats crossing to Dublin each week, taking with them the mail. These boats ran on Mondays, Wednesdays and Fridays and return trips were made with the Irish Mail on Sundays, Wednesdays and Fridays. Journey time averaged twelve hours for one crossing, although the shortest was only six (it is now only one and a half hours!). Wind, it goes without saying, is extremely flighty hereabout, and journey times were wholly dependent on this inconsistency. The basic ferry crossing cost one guinea. For some strange reason, it is said that Holyhead's bread came across on the ferry from Ireland!

Although Holyhead was recognised as a harbour before Lewis Morris arrived, he suggested the building of more piers, one of which was to connect Salt Island with the mainland. He also recognised that if the harbour was repaired and warehouses built, then the Irish might come over to trade their goods. These suggested improvements, he estimated, would cost between four and five thousand pounds. The port might have been in some sort of decline at that time as nothing happened.

In 1747, Morris notes that 22,000 bushels (a bushel being eight gallons) of grain were shipped out, mostly to Ireland, I suspect. The other commodities of the port were much the same as the rest of Anglesey, such as butter, cheese and bacon. No mention was made of salted herring. He did note wild fowl, kelp and sampier, a well-known pickle found on the cliffs of nearby Holyhead Mountain (Mynydd Twr). As to fish, it seems that there were plentiful supplies of 'Oysters, Lobsters, Crabs, Razor-fish, Shrimps, Herrings, Cod-fish, Whiting, Whiting Pollacks, Blackings, Sea Trench, Turbot, Soles, Flounders, Rays and other Fish'. There was obviously no shortage of fishing here, but little is known about the antics of the fishermen and how they caught this fish. One or two drawings show small open boats with a small lugsail, that were probably similar to the boats of the north coast of the island, sailing about the harbour.

Morris goes on to identify the salt-house on which 'an Act passed the 6th of Queen Anne, to permit Rock Salt to be used here, to strengthen Sea Water'. It seems that salt was manufactured from the sea water, with rock salt being added to improve the flavour. This fell into decay after the management failed to oversee its success, though not before a substantial amount of salt was smuggled in from the Isle of Man so as to avoid the hated salt tax.

Salt was an important commodity in medieval times. The storage of meat and fish relied upon salt as a preservative in those days. Hanging in the fireplace in the smoke was also found to help preservation. In time salting methods improved, and both beef and herring were salted down in barrels and exported. Although the true kipper didn't arrive until the nineteenth century, it may be presumed that some form of smoked herring had been eaten for centuries.

Taxes were introduced on salt in the late seventeenth century as a means of raising funds for overseas wars. Smuggling was the only means of avoiding the unjust costs, and the same became true during the next century as a means of avoiding the crippling taxes that were imposed on luxury goods. Although salt is believed to have been the first smuggling commodity, tea, brandy and tobacco soon became more profiterable for the 'free traders'. In many coastal areas smuggling was assumed to be a lawful pastime and that taxes were totally unjustified. There are many anecdotes about local magistrates informing the smugglers of the imminent arrival of the revenue men, for which they were rewarded with a barrel of brandy outside their backdoor that evening.

Salt, in the eighteenth century, cost four pennies a pound in Wales after the dreaded salt tax was added. Ports even had a Salt Officer to oversee the payment of taxes on landed salt. However, across the Irish Sea, the same amount of salt cost only one penny. Wasn't it then reasonable to buy smuggled salt for two pennies a pound, especially when it was considered as a basic necessity to store food for the winter? I would certainly say so! Many a dark night saw barrels of salt landed on the quiet coves along the coast of Anglesey, some even coming from the Isle of Man. The practise continued until the repeal of the salt taxes in the first part of the nineteenth century.

Returning to the port of Holyhead, it is worth noting that the seafront was a hive of shipbuilding activity in the eighteenth and nineteenth centuries, with various boats being built at any one time upon the slipways that adorned the area. Boats of up to two hundred tons could be accommodated, and vessels from all over the west coast came here for repairs. The breakwater, for which Holyhead is renowned, is the longest in the country and was designed by James Meadows Rendal in 1845. Work began on the one and a half mile (2.4km) structure two years later, but it wasn't completed until 1873 and had cost £1,285,000 in total. Rendal had died in 1856, supposedly from natural causes, although rumour suggested suicide because his original design had been altered so much: the designed 5360 feet (1631m) North Pier had increased to 7860 feet (2395m), and his East and Mail Packet piers were never built at all.

Today's fishing quay lies largely empty, although it has recently been moved and refurbished. Sadly few boats land here, although at times some of the west coast fleet do use the excellent facilities. Even fewer local boats are based here, and over the last few years, several boats have been decommissioned and unceremoniously burnt nearby. This process of scrapping perfectly good vessels has been happening all over Britain as the country's fishing industry is, piece by piece, being dismantled by our politicians to appease our European brothers as part of the chess game of dialogue and favours. Britain once had some 65% of Europe's fishing grounds within its territorial waters, but on entry to the club in the early 1970s, this was immediately deemed negotiable. So began the programme of giving access to other members that has, twenty-five years later, resulted in substantial hardship to fishing communities and individuals, especially those from the coastal fishing sector who have relied upon this unwritten right to take fish from the sea for generations. They have used methods of fishing that date back a long way, but are now largely ignored by the authorities. Only those with the power of the bankers behind them can set sail in vast technologically perfect catching-boats that sweep up as many fish as possible; these coastal folk with their smaller, older, less-efficient fishing boats are encouraged to chop them up into firewood and call it a day. Each big monster employs a few fishermen, but can catch an amount of fish that probably ten times the crew numbers would have only dreamt of catching a hundred years ago. Possibly even more. The rest have only the dole to look forward to as these changes, that we are told represent the better side of progression, take place.

It is not a pleasant sight seeing a wooden fishing boat being pulled apart by a JCB. I recently watched the process in Cornwall, where the fishermen have perhaps experienced more hardship than most. The boat, with all its useful gear removed, is taken alongside the quay, and attacked by the machine as it hacks its way into the innards. The whole boat shudders as each movement of the jib tears away a splinter of wood. Only one thing is obvious, and that is that these craft are strongly built and have nowhere nearly reached the end of their useful life. It can take a whole week to dismantle the vessel and cart the pieces away to be burnt. On other occasions boats have been dumped in tips and smashed up, others have been chainsawed up, and others set alight on beaches. Many a grown man has been reduced to tears watching the tool of his livelihood being thus disposed of. It has been called 'legalised vandalism' by the 40+ Fishing Boat Association, that has fought hard to prevent this destruction, while it is all done in the so called name of conservation. The unfortunate trend throughout our modern society is to take out the small operator and let the big ones have a clear run.

Holyhead did once thrive as a fishing port. In the early part of the twentieth century herring boats from Ireland, the Isle of Man and Scotland came here to land their substantial catches and the herring lassies – the roving bands of Scots girls that followed the herring fleets all over Britain to gut and barrel the fish – worked tirelessly at their troughs of herring, gutting up to sixty fish a minute and packing them into the barrels that stood alongside them. These were then taken to the railway for shipment all over Europe. In the previous century salted herring was sent to the West Indies to feed the slaves until slavery was abolished in 1834; to Russia and Germany to satiate an endless market; and it was used to supplement the diet of the British army and navy in their endless battles around the globe as Britain preserved and extended its Empire in distant lands.

Although the First World War brought about a severe decline in the trade, Holyhead did enjoy a brief respite in the 1930s when the west coast boats landed their catches in the port. Another upsurge in the fortunes of the fishermen occurred in the 1950s when the herring industry again flourished for a short period, when large amounts of herring were cured on Salt Island, but afterwards the fishing trade plunged into a decline from which it has never really emerged.

Unknown to many is the fact that Holyhead benefited from whaling in the 1930s. During the depression, when about one third of the Holyhead workforce were out of work, forty-four Anglesey men were chosen to work aboard the whalers *Southern Princess* and *Southern Empress*, which took them on in Liverpool. Owned by the Southern Whaling & Sealing Company, these boats sailed to the Antarctic for the summer season in 1936, catching whales of all species.

During a trip that lasted from about the beginning of December to mid-March, the men were paid £9 10s a month, with bonuses for overtime of 1 shilling an hour and a sum per barrel of whale oil and liver flakes that were produced. As the average wage in the town was a mere £2 a week, arriving home with £100 or more was an enormous boost to both the town and the men. More

Holyhead men went out the next year, and one hundred and twenty-three in 1938, when the combined number of barrels of oil brought back by both ships was 210,000. Another group went in 1939 as war was beginning to break out, and a secret trip was arranged the following year that appears to have been the final one.

They caught all sorts of whales and used the whole carcass during the process, not wasting anything. The blubber was sliced off to be ground up and then boiled; the skeletons were also boiled, under pressure, and the liver was minced and dried into flakes. This last process was the most profiterable part of the whole exercise, and the crews believed that the whole trip was paid for out of the proceeds of the liver flakes. The rest was pure profit for the company.

The story of whaling is perhaps one lasting sad instance of mankind's excesses. Originally stemming from the need for oil to burn in the lamps needed to light up our streets, and later for soap manufacturing and margarine making, forty thousand whales were killed around the Antarctic in 1930 alone. Conservation wasn't on the agenda then, although concern was being voiced about the number being killed. There were about thirty fleets working there until the onset of world war in 1939. War allowed the stocks a chance to recover briefly, but whaling resumed soon after the end, and with a vengeance. By the 1950s the whole area was overfished and, with the setting up of the International Whaling Commission in 1949, recognition of this slowly filtered through to the politicians. However, by this time, the boats had become massive industrial ships that managed to plunder the area of blue and fin whales (the most valuable because of their size) and many other species. Politicians alone couldn't stem this greed, and it wasn't until the companies themselves began to realise in the 1960s that they were catching fewer whales, of which a large proportion were immature, that they began to see for themselves that something was up. Restrictions and zero quotas were enforced, and later a moratorium was imposed which largely remains today, except where Norway and Japan insist in taking whales for 'scientific purposes'. Few doubt the reasoning behind this as, in 1998, these 'researchers' sold their catch in Japanese fish markets for an estimates US$50 million, according to Greenpeace sources. Since Antarctica was made a whale sanctuary by the IWC in 1994, some 1,648 whales have been killed there.

A lifeboat was established in Holyhead in 1828, the second lifeboat to be initially stationed on Ynys Môn. Although the design was the same as that at Cemlyn, this one was built by the boatbuilder Henry McVeagh of the town. A steam lifeboat was stationed here in 1890, with a sailing boat kept in reserve. The first motor lifeboat was brought on station in 1922, and the port remains one of the main lifeboat stations around this part of the coast.

Signs of the tramway that was used to transport stone from the quarry on Holyhead Mountain down and along the breakwater during its construction can still be seen. Below, the coves around Porth-y-felin are homes to several fishing craft that rarely seem to go to sea. The coastal footpath runs along the tramway for a while, and can be followed indistinctly up to the quarries. From there the path leads up to North Stack (Ynys Arw) where spectacular views can be had over the cliffs and surrounding area, as well as over towards the north-west of Anglesey and the Skerries and down to the Llŷn peninsula in the opposite direction.

South Stack (Ynys Lawd), where a light has shone since 1809, lies at the other end of Gogarth Bay. As the Welsh name states, it is an island, with some three hundred and something steps leading down to a suspension bridge which can sometimes be crossed to view the island and its famous light. From the cliff above the island, the road and footpath can be walked to Porth Ruffydd on the southern side of the Caergybi headland, where a lifeboat was established between 1891 and 1903. An iron age fort sat atop a rocky stack just offshore at one time.

Porth Dafarch is a sandy beach a mile to the east of Porth Ruffydd. Although favoured by holiday-makers, divers and pleasure boat users, this unlikely setting was at one time where the sailing packets from Ireland landed when adverse winds in Holyhead harbour made it inaccessible. On this tiny beach passengers were transferred into and from ships that sailed across the blue-grey sea. Holyhead didn't always have the exclusive right to embarking people to Ireland. Indeed in the early nineteenth century some planned that Porthdinllaen, ỏn the northern side of the Llŷn peninsula and some twenty-one miles due south, would become the main embarkation port for the Irish packet. Although hope seemed to last for the whole century that perhaps one day a service could be successfully entertained over to Dublin, it wasn't until the early twentieth century that the plans at Porth Dinllaen were finally buried.

Trearddur Bay was once a small hamlet from where several lobster boats worked this coast. However, with its growth into a visitor's paradise and holidaying centre, with caravans and bungalows owned mostly by the rich middle-class from the Liverpool and Manchester areas, the whole balance in the village altered. By the 1950s there appeared to be only one full-time lobster fisherman who worked some twenty pots between mid-May and mid-September. In the ensuing years several part-timers joined in, although temporarily, and today the holiday-makers probably illegally catch more fish than do the locals legally.

The housing about this part of the coast is most unsympathetic to the island's considerations. They are strange buildings that are totally out of place amongst the traditional dwellings of the area. With their weird roof-lines, obscenely large windows and unnecessarily grandiose structures, it really does amaze me how they were ever given permission to be erected. The same can be said for some of the intruding caravans that surround otherwise beautiful bays, thereby excluding the local people from enjoying those particular beaches. Nowhere else on Anglesey is the anglicisation of the community as apparent as it is here.

There's a pleasant walk from here over the clifftop to

Rhoscolyn, a perfectly sheltered beach on the southern edge of Holy Island (Ynys Cybi). There was a healthy oyster fishery here at the end of the nineteenth century. Small boats, strongly built, were used to dredge the oysters that lay a few miles offshore. These were then brought ashore and laid upon the beach below the highwater mark so that they could mature in size. Once big enough, they were loaded into sloops and taken by sea to Liverpool. However, the trade ceased before the turn of the century as larger beds superceeded the smaller ones, and pollution caused many a scare that affected oyster eating. Today, with oysters fetching high prices, it's hard to realise that they were eaten widely throughout Britain and weren't regarded as much of a delicacy as they are now. It's a bit like the salmon that once caused the servant classes working in many a stately home to go on strike against eating the fish more than three days a week! Salmon largely replaced herring as the staple diet fish of the country. Ironically, it was while attempting to experiment with the smoking of salmon that John Woodger first discovered, so it is said, the secret of smoking herrings into kippers in 1843.

There's still a lifeboat house on the western edge of the beach. A lifeboat was first stationed here in 1831 built, as the one in Holyhead, by Henry McVeagh. A boat remained based here until its closure in 1929. Tragically, one lifeboat was lost here with all hands during an attempt to save the crew of the SS Timbo in 1920.

One particular fisherman is remembered here for his gallant rescues to vessels in distress. The treacherous

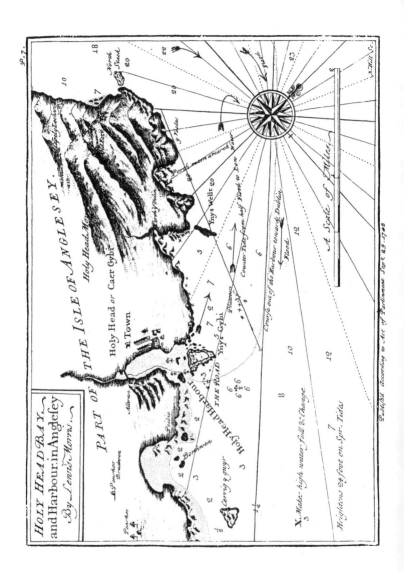

HOLY HEAD BAY, and Harbour, in Anglesey By Lewis Morris.

PART OF THE ISLE OF ANGLESEY.

A Scale of Miles.

Publish'd according to Act of Parliament Sep. 29. 1748.

The fish trap at Beaumaris life boat house in the 1950's
(photo: Bridget Dempsey)

The same fish trap showing the 'crew' where the bulk of the fish were trapped
(photo: Bridget Dempsey)

Beaumaris lifeboat station. Built in 1914 alongside the fishtrap, the station was closed in 1991 and demolished a few months later.
(photo: Bridget Dempsey)

A good catch of lobsters c.1950!
(photo: Bridget Dempsey)

Detail of the fish trap walls
(photo: Bridget Dempsey)

John Girling showing his catch of (mainly) mackerel with a good salmon thrown in
(photo: Bridget Dempsey)

Brothers Wilf and John Girling displaying the day's catch c.1960
(photo: Bridget Dempsey)

John Girling (senior) with a landing–net full of whitebait
(photo: Bridget Dempsey)

Stephenson's Britannia bridge was built in 1850. More recently it's been strengthened to carry the main Holyhead trunk road.
(photo: Author's collection)

rocks that extend more than half a mile offshore from here have caught many an unsuspecting ship. Huw Hughes used his own small open fishing boat, and sometimes those of his fellow fishers, to save some one hundred and two lives over a period of fifteen years towards the end of the nineteenth century, venturing out on no less than eight occassions in adverse conditions. Huw later became the coxswain of the Rhoscolyn lifeboat.

There isn't a public right of way along the coast eastwards from Rhoscolyn, although there is a tiny path over to Porth Gorslwyn. However there is a right of way from the roadway to Traeth Llydan (Silver Sands), a wonderful beach at the northern edge of Cymyran Bay. This lies at the southern entrance of the creek that separates Holy Island from the rest of Anglesey and eventually opens up into the Inland Sea. The only way of traversing this water is by retracing northwards and crossing over the stone bridge at Rhyd-bont (Fourmile Bridge).

Chapter 6

From Lobsters to Lovers

Llanddwyn Twr Mawr lighthouse '99

While traversing the bridge across the creek, it's worth noting that several small open craft are normally moored to the south. It's easy to imagine the same scene a hundred years ago with several fishing craft anchored there.

The whole of the area from here to Cymyran dries out to a narrow channel at low water, and although most of the sands can be walked upon, it's best to keep to the coastal path unless one has local knowledge. A good eye must be kept on the tide in any case as, at high water, the whole area becomes a different place.

Cymyran itself, hardly more than a few buildings, lies on the Anglesey side at the southern entrance to the creek. Here one or two fishermen worked 18 feet (5.5m) open boats with up to fifty pots in the 1950s. However the whole section of the beach here is somewhat smothered by the RAF base at Valley (Dyffryn). Indeed many spectators gather in the car park to watch the fighter planes practise their take-off and landing skills, whizzing up above their heads, destroying whatever peace there was before. The base was opened in 1941, and had been built on more than one half of Tywyn Trewan Common, an extensive peaty marshland that is now covered in sand that has been swept in by the combined action of the sea and wind. However, it mustn't be forgotten that the RAF 22 Squadron Air-Sea Rescue helicopters are also based here. These helicopters are scrambled at a moment's notice to go immediately to the aid of anyone, whethere at sea or on land, and many fisherman has had cause to rely upon their services.

The coastal footpath follows the beach for nearly two miles, crossing the small river via a footbridge a little upstream so as to arrive in Rhosneigr. However, during the walk over the sands, it is worth reflecting on the fact that, given that the overhead planes are a nuisance, plans were prepared around the turn of the century to build an ammunition factory all over the common, with jobs for over 300 people. The plans were opposed by the hoteliers of Rhosneigr so that the factory was never built.

Afon Crigyll, just crossed, was once navigable about one mile upstream, and was once central to the small settlement here. The Lladron Crigyll (Crigyll wreckers) lured ships onto the rocky shore here, plundering the booty and hiding it amongst the dunes. Three men were committed for trial at Beaumaris Gaol in 1715 and were found guilty of the raiding of the sloop *The Charming Jenny* that was stranded in the river.

Rhosneigr has been renowned for its lobsters for generations. As far back as 1600 George Roberts noted that the lobsters there were 'very sweete and delicate meate and plentie taken'. Until the 1880s, it was a tiny sleepy village of scattered white cottages whose inhabitants survived from catching lobsters in the summer, and sending them to distant markets. Boats came to the beach so as to load them, bringing with in coal and limestone. Butter, cheese and corn were exported as well as lobsters, and the village was largely self-sufficient for much of its needs. During the summer large catches of mackerel were taken here, and this continues on a smaller scale even today. Good catches of whiting, plaice, bream, conger eel, seatrout and prawns were reported in the early part of the twentieth century. Herring, it seems, was hardly ever landed here as it was generally scarce on the west of Anglesey, due to the stronger tides.

The first of the visitors came in the 1880s, encouraged by the fact that the village had a small station on the main Holyhead railway. Their arrival heralded an abrupt change from the traditional way of life. They came and built houses to use in the summer, enjoying the lovely beaches that the west coast was renowned for. The hoteliers arrived too, to build their hotels – the same people who successfully challenged the building of the armaments factory, such was their influence further afield.

The first study of lobster fishing in North Wales was made by Rev William Bingley in 1800 who wrote that 'collecting lobsters and crabs occupies most of the time of the inhabitants of Bardsey Island'. Bardsey is Ynys Enlli, and lies off the extreme end of the Llŷn peninsula. In all probability, the Rhosneigr men relied upon the lobsters as much as the men of Ynys Enlli. Bingley goes on to say that the pots were 'made of willows exactly in the shape of a wire mouse trap, with the cone inverted'. These pots, otherwise known as ink-well pots, originated supposedly from a Cornish design, although the fishermen of North Devon have also used them for generations. The Clovelly fishermen used to go up into the woods above the village, out of the fishing season, and spend several days collecting willow, which they would gather and take home to make their own pots.

Today lobster fishing is largely a thing of the past, although several holiday-makers who come to the village each year, bringing along a boat, often set a few pots offshore to catch lobsters for their dinner. When I was a child I remember going out with several pots, setting them with a brick and maybe a couple of mackerel heads in as bait. It was, however, a rare occurrence to return the next day to find a lobster, let alone two! It seems that lobsters prefer salted gurnard to a measely mackerel head!

Rhosneigr lobstermen used open boats of about 15 feet (5m) in length that had a small transom stern. Transom sterns were favoured by such fishermen because it gave them added buoyancy at the aft end, which in turn allowed them greater safety when hauling the pots up. Larger boats can haul over one side – modern boats usually have a winch on one side to bring them up much quicker – but smaller boats tend to capsize when the fisherman leans over too far. Double-ended boats were traditionally favoured by fisherman with sails – probably due to the Viking influence upon these coasts in the ninth and tenth centuries when they arrived in their Norse double-enders. The same evolution is apparent all around the north coast of Britain, while those on the south coast often favoured the transom after French influence. The traditional fishing boats of Aberdaron make a good example. In the nineteenth century they had pointed sterns from when they were catching large amounts of herring. Once the herring declined, they concentrated on lobster fishing for a living, and within a decade they began to build boats with the transom stern for increased safety at sea. Several fishermen, it seems, were drowned while hauling up their pots over the side.

Twenty pots was the average number for Rhosneigr fishermen, and they would haul them each day except Saturdays and Sundays, re-baiting them with the salted gurnard and removing any lobster. Crabs didn't like the salted fish and preferred fresher morsels, although some were caught and sold. Into the twentieth century an annual catch of four hundred lobsters was regarded as about average, with the average weight of each lobster being nearly two pounds 0.9kg.

Rhosneigr had its own lifeboat house which was built in 1872 at a cost of £680, the money coming from the wife of Thomas Lingham who was drowned nearby. In all there were three boats stationed there up until the station's closure in 1924, all of which were named *Thomas Lingham*. During this period it managed to save seventy-three lives on being launched twenty-nine times. Perhaps the most famous of its launches was to the *Norman Castle* in 1883, when it tried in vain to reach the ship that was stranded in Cymyran Bay. By chance the Rhoscolyn lifeboat was in Porth Dafarch, having sustained damage the previous day. The Rhosneigr boat tried several times to get close to the stricken boat, but was eventually driven ashore with an exhausted crew. The Holyhead lifeboat crew then arrived, brought in by train, and they succeeded in rescuing all of the crew of the ship, after re-launching the Rhosneigr boat into the surf.

South of Rhosneigr, Traeth Llydan stretches for a mile southwards and is as perfect a beach as can be found anywhere with sand-dunes backing onto the hinterland. Porth Nobla is a small beach at the southern end which is a perfect spot for an evening swim. The coastal footpath follows the edge of the sand-dunes. On the headland at the extreme end is situated the burial chambers of Barclodiad y Gawres which date back to the Neolithic age. Porth Trecastell – sometimes called Cable Bay because of the underwater telegraph that once led from here over to Ireland – is half-hidden beyond the headland. Smugglers and pirates once worked off the beach here, and it is said that lanterns were tied onto the horns of cattle so that ships out in the bay would mistake these lights for other ships and sail towards them, thereby driving themselves directly onto the rocks each side of the beach. The boats were then plundered in the same way as Lladron Crigyll worked off the beach at Rhosneigr. However, it must be said that the story of lanterns on cattle and such pirating is told in many other regions of Britain! A smuggler's boat, called the *Fox*, worked this coast in the mid-eighteenth century. Crewed by a bunch of ruthless firebrands, they landed tobacco, brandy, wine, tea and geneva gin directly onto the beach for distribution around the community.

Between here and Porth Cwyfan there is no coastal path because of the disused old army camp and the danger area from where missiles were once fired out to sea. To walk to this bay with the little church on the island, it is necessary to walk along the road and down a footpath that leads directly to the beach.

The small church was founded in the seventh century by St Cwyfan and is connected to the shore by a causeway at low tide. Despite being restored twice in the intervening period, the layout of the church has survived much the same. The gravestone of Frank Morley Churnley, a 20 year old who was drowned at Porth Trecastell in 1869, stands alone in the graveyard.

From here, retracing one's steps back to the beach, the coastal footpath can be walked along towards Aberffraw. The path here is just yards away from the ever impatient sea, passing Porth Aels with its iron winch that stands upon the cliff, before going up to the headland of Carreg Foel with its spectacular views over the dramatic beach of Aberffraw – Traeth Mawr – and beyond to the mountains of Snowdonia.

Aberffraw was once another sleepy village with white cottages overlooking the sea, that survived chiefly from fishing. Aberffraw was also the administrative centre of a vast portion of North Wales, and at times of Wales, for over eight hundred years until the thirteenth century. The Irish raided the place in 962, the consequences of which are largely unknown, although it is known that they partially destroyed the king's palace. Later on, before the estuary was silted up by sand, the village was a busy port with ships calling in from far afield. In more recent times sloops sailed up the river to load up with the local produce of butter, cheese and corn, according to Lewis Morris. He suggested the building of a pier some twenty or so yards long to make it a good harbour. Strangely enough, the report prepared for the North Wales Development Council in 1947 suggested exactly the same thing, and in nearly the exact same words. Morris found oysters, whiting and other fish in plenty, and the sand was noted for its good manuring qualities, like that of Traeth Coch (Red Wharf Bay). An herring fishery was established here briefly in 1884 when huge shoals visited this part of the coast. This was largely exploited by the fishermen and merchants of Liverpool, with hardly any fish being landed in the village, and hence the villagers had no advantage from the fishery. Like other parts of Anglesey, shipbuilding flourished in the estuary in the late eighteenth century.

Between Aberffraw and Malltraeth, much of the coast is owned by the Bodorgan Estates, and access to the coast is unfortunately prohibited at present. However I did recently walk along the foreshore at low tide to the old fish house at Porth Melin, under Dinas Llwyd. This attractive little stone building was once used by fishermen who undoubtedly fished off the nearby beach. Inside, remnants of a fishing age adorn the shelves, although I'm assured by the estate that today it is never used. Funny that the newspapers were only a month old! Sitting in the autumnal evening sun, throwing stones for the dog, I couldn't help but feel that this spot was ideal for the landing of salmon and other fish, and could easily imagine the fishermen sitting around the ancient wooden table yarning and waiting for the tide. The Estate papers show that a salmon fishing licence was bought in 1884 but not in subsequent years. Previously, salmon was bought in at 2 shillings a pound and 30 fresh herring for 5d in 1700. Mystery, therefore, surrounds this building, although it has been suggested that it was a mill before being used by local fishermen.

Malltraeth, like Aberffraw, is a small village sitting by the side of a river that flows out into a large estuary, in this case Afon Cefni. Ships were built here at the end of the eighteenth century. At that time the sea flowed nearly as far as Llangefni in the middle of the island – a little like Aberffraw where the sea flowed much further inland until the formation of sand-dunes forced it back. In Malltraeth the hinterland was reclaimed by the building of the cob, which was completed in 1811. Fishing was not an important economic feature here, although Lewis Morris reported that 'most kind of Fish' were in plentiful supply. Cockles abounded at low water, and mussels were picked here. Some continue to be so taken, but only on a small scale. Oysters were also cultured here at one time, so it is said, but pollution and over fishing soon caused problems and the oysters are extremely rare these days.

Morris advocated the building of two piers, one at Dinas Llwyd on the northern side of the entrance to the estuary, and another under Bodorgan for the coal barges (the North Wales Development Council made exactly the same suggestion again). Coal was exported from the mines under Malltraeth Marsh. It was this coal, you will remember, that was to be taken by rail to Porth Llongdy at Traeth Coch under the proposed 1812 railway scheme. Morris also suggested that the entrance of the estuary could completely be closed off, thereby converting the whole bay eventually to meadow, and forming an excellent harbour at the entrance in the process. Nothing was ever done, as in Aberffraw, so that it remains as it has done for centuries, quiet and devoid of industry except for agriculture.

It's a wonderful walk, first along the cob with wildlife on both sides, and then along the edge of the estuary just within Newborough forest. The forest is of a formidable size, given that fifty years ago it was just a huge expanse of sand-dunes. Today it produces some ten thousand tons of timber annually. In much earlier times, Neolithic man lived here and relics from his past have been discovered, including mounds of edible mollusc shells. The path winds through the forest and eventually emerges on one of the most beautiful beaches on Anglesey, Traeth Penrhos. Walking along the edge of this beach for a mile brings the walker to Ynys Llanddwyn.

Upon the island, which is only detached from the main island on spring tides, is the church of St Dwynwen, who came here in about the fifth century after a failed affair of the heart with a prince named Maelon. She desired solitude amongst the dunes and the sea. Her nearby well of miraculous waters allowed hopeful lovers to ascertain the depth of their partner's faithfulness towards them, with a little bit of help from a sacred eel who lived in the well. Word spread quickly of this soucerous spot and visitors soon came from every direction. Today the well is said to exist but I can't find it, and supposedly the eel still lives within its dark depths.

St Dwynwen then became the patron saint of Welsh lovers, and her little church grew as a place of pilgrimage. Today little remains, and what does suggests late fifteenth to early sixteenth century construction. It has been said that the locals removed much of the church timbers to use for boatbuilding nearly two hundred years ago. A service once a year keeps alive the religous tradition here.

Pilot's Cove, at the extreme tip of the island, was formed in the early nineteenth century when a causeway was built to connect up a closeby islet. Cottages were built for salvageman who would go out to help stricken ship. Caernarfon Bar, with its shallow channel and constantly-shifting sandbanks, was a notorious place for such incidents, and consequently a lifeboat station was established in 1840. The lifeboat house still remains, although this was built later on, in 1861. A new boat was delivered in 1885, but the service was finally withdrawn in 1907. The lifeboat coxswain was the chief pilot and he lived in one of the cottages. The rest of the crew lived in nearby Newborough and were summoned to duty by the firing of a cannon. Later on, two more cottages were built and Llanddwyn became a recognised pilot station where a pilot could be taken aboard by vessels heading up the channel into Caernarfon or Felinheli (Port Dinorwig), both of which were by this time busy ports that were chiefly engaged in the slate trade.

At the beginning of the nineteenth century a white stone tower (Tŵr Bach) was erected close to Pilot's Cove, but this was deemed difficult to identify when making towards the bar. A larger stone tower (Tŵr Mawr) was then built slightly to the west in 1846, and this had a red oil lamp that was illuminated at night. Both towers remain, although the light was moved in 1972 to the top of the original Tŵr Bach and is now automatic.

It's again a wonderful walk along the beach of Llanddwyn Bay, in the shadow of the forest. After a mile or so the forest ends, and Tywyn Niwbwrch (Newborough Warren) continues over the sand-dunes. The remains of the original village of Rhosyr that consisted of eight messuages' in 1305 can still be seen on the mainland. The village was overcome by sand during a particularly severe storm on St Nicholas Day in 1330.

The whole coast is on the move here because of erosion from the wind and sea. This was one reason for planting the forest in the 1950s. Marram grass had been planted centuries before to help bind the sand, and this gave rise to a thriving basket-making industry in nearby Newborough. Ever since the sixteenth century, the people of the village cut the grass and made ropes, baskets and mats in a cottage industry. The produce was sold around the markets of the island and over the water in the weekly Caernarfon market, until the trade faded in the first half of the twentieth century as cheap imports removed the markets and the cost of collecting the grass increased. Until the nineteenth century Newborough Warren was common land, but it then passed into private hands with the Land Enclosure Acts. From that time, rents had to be paid for the right to the grass from individual plots that, before the Enclosure Acts, had been owned by no man, and had been free for the taking. The village was once described as 'the most miserable spot on Anglesey', and it was said of the people that 'to fill them there was no food but only the sad harvest of the beach'. Yet they produced all manner of goods from their industry to give them a living, albeit at a subsistence level. It was still an industry that allowed the village to survive the great hardships that came with the new Industrial Age in many other parts of the country.

It is possible to walk to the extreme south-west tip of Anglesey at Trwyn Abermenai, from where a ferry once ran over to mainland Wales that was often used by the Newborough folk to take their wares to Caernarfon. It is a very pleasant walk through the sand-dunes or along the beach to this remote spot. In the shelter of the lee of the spit, several fishing boats were moored in the nineteenth century. Fishing, though, was largely foresaken along this portion of the Anglesey coast.

Perhaps the pilots of Llanddwyn fished from their small boats or directly off the rocks to supplement their diet. However it's a very uncertain coast, with strong tides and a seemingly eternal wind that make it quite dangerous for small boats because of the lack of shelter from the elements. Nearby Caernarfon had a fleet of fishing boats, and some three hundred were registered there in 1883. Many of these, although registered in the town, were based further along the coast at villages such as Nefyn where a very healthy herring fishery thrived, with curing houses established on the shore, into the twentieth century. Nefyn herring were very popular throughout North and Mid Wales because of their superb taste.

The Torbay system of trawling was introduced into Caernarfon Bay by a Mr O. Williams of Llanidan at the beginning of the nineteenth century, and later Conwy Bay and Traeth Coch. This brought a big influx of fishing boats from Liverpool and Dublin and commercial fishing, as we've already seen in the case of the brief herring fishery at Aberffraw, was often controlled by these outsiders. The locals were happy to catch enough for their own needs, but were not keen to increase the taking of fish from their waters. Time has proven them correct in their assumptions as it was the Torbay trawl that was ultimately responsible for the over-fishing that has ravaged stocks over the last one hundred years.

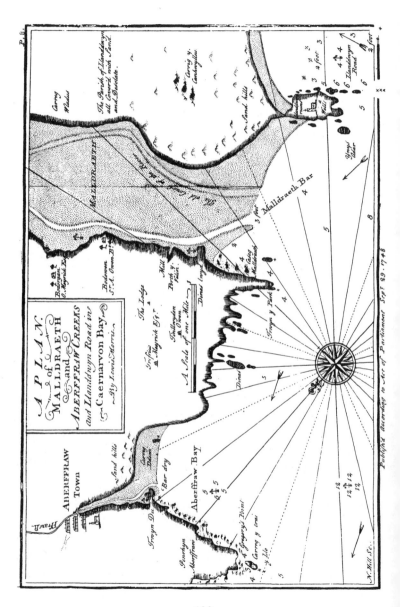

A PLAN
of
MALLDRAETH
and
ABERFFRAW CREEKS
and Llanidwyn Road in
Caernarvon Bay
By Lewis Morris

ABERFFRAW
Town

Aberffraw Bay

Malldraeth Bar

The Parish of Llanidwyn, all Cover'd with Sand, and Desolate.

Published according to Act of Parliament Sept. 29, 1748.

120

Chapter 7

Fishweirs for Whitebait Teas

Long Ship Inn was an ancient pub, so it is said, on the edge of Newborough Warren, close to the mouth of Afon Braint. The fishermen supposedly moored their boats in a deeper part of the river, where it turns ninety degrees and has formed a bit of a bowl, and then they walked up towards Newborough, calling at the pub on the way as it was situated at the bottom of Pen-lôn.

Walking along the Menai Strait from this point is not easy, although it is perfectly possible with local knowledge. Alternatively, from the main road above Pen-lôn, there is a footpath that follows a lane down to the stepping stones over Afon Braint and then along the river, before veering right across fields and eventually to the road that goes down to the beach at Borth. Caernarfon, with its well-preserved castle, lies across the water. Two hundred yards along the beach in the direction of Trwyn Abermenai there is a small harbour that once belonged to the 'big house' nearby, into where small sloops came bringing coal and limestone and exporting the local produce.

It is possible to walk in the other direction along the stony beach to the Mermaid Inn, although this is not a public right of way. However, beware of doing this at or near high water as the water's edge comes right up to the sandstone cliff at times. The inn used to be called the Menai hotel, and is sited above the high water jetty that was used for the ferry across to Caernarfon. This is the Tal-y-foel ferry which ran at least since the thirteenth century when it was used to carry stones for the building of Caernarfon castle. Records of the passenger ferry didn't commence until 1425.

Over the years a considerable number of drownings have occurred during accidents to the ferryboat. Seventy-nine people were killed in 1664 when it capsized, and another thirty people were lost in 1723. In 1785 the Abermenai ferry hit the sandbank and was swamped by the rough sea near Caernarfon and fifty-four folk were drowned. One man, Huw Williams, survived. The last disaster involved another Huw Williams being the sole survivor when the rival ferry from Barras – half a mile up the seafront from the Mermaid – capsized in 1820 and twenty-two people

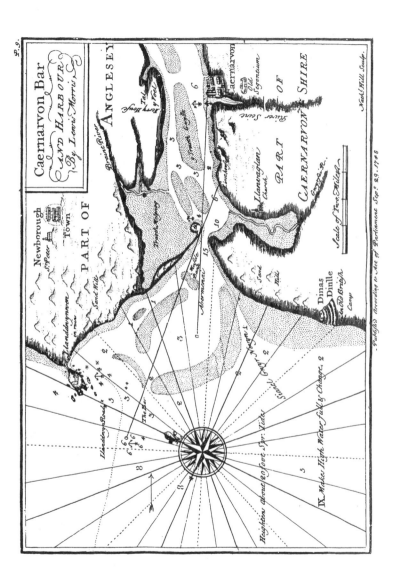

Caernarvon Bar
AND HARBOUR
By Lewis Morris

ANGLESEY

PART OF

Newborough Town

PART OF CAERNARVON SHIRE

Caernarvon

Published According to Act of Parliament Sep.r 29. 1748

died. The ferry finally closed down in 1953 because of quicker forms of transport. Once a bus service was started between Newborough and Caernarfon, the ferry became superfluous.

The low water jetty still stands on the beach one hundred yards or so along the seafront. The old co-op, where local produce was sold, stands on the corner of the road, albeit now converted into dwellings.

Fish have never been taken here in quantity, although the writer does remember laying small nets on the beach many years ago, and finding mullet, pollack and other small fish in them. Mussels lie on the beach, seeded in the last century. Although we used to pick them thirty years ago, today they are licensed to fishermen for their sole use. Oysters more recently have been laid on the beach to grow, but these are again privately owned and should be left well alone.

Although not wishing to publicise the tourist attractions of Ynys Môn, it's worth noting that the Anglesey Sea Zoo have their aquarium just along the seafront. This is a dynamic display of many of the native fish found in the waters around Anglesey.

There's a footpath that runs from the beach at Barras to Llanidan, Porth-aml and by road to Moel-y-don. Ships of over one hundred tons were built here in the closing years of the eighteenth century. Here, too, was a ferry crossing point to Felinheli (Port Dinorwig), where slate from the nearby Dinorwig mines of Llanberis was brought by rail for loading onto ships in the inner basin. This ferry was used by the men of Brynsiencyn who worked in the mines. They left on a Monday morning, not to return until the end of the week.

The estate of the Marquis of Anglesey, Plas Newydd, blocks the way eastwards from here, for the walker at least, and has to be circumvented by road. The next quay along is at Pwllfanog which was a flourishing small harbour until about 1900, engaged in exporting slate for school writing tablets and milled flour. There was a margarine factory and a bacon factory in operation here in more recent times. The quay is said to date back to thte sixteenth century, and there have been suggestions of a dock on the opposite side of the Strait.

Stephenson's Britannia Bridge is nearby. Originally built as a tubular bridge to carry the railway, it was badly damaged by fire on 23 May 1970 and was subsequently re-built with a new roadway suspended over the original rail platform. From the roadway there's a superb view in both directions along the Strait, although pedestrians are not encouraged.

Telford's Suspension Bridge is a mile (1.5km) eastwards, and the piece of water between the two bridges is known as Pwll Ceris (or the Swellies). Here the tide flows strongly over the rocks in the narrow channel, and these create overfalls and eddies that can be extremely treacherous to shipping.

Lewis Morris recognised this, describing it as 'a dangerous Part of the Straits of Menai'. He mentions the great overfalls, violent currents and whirlpools on both the flood and ebb tides, which make this section of the Strait one of the most perilous streches of water on the west coast, unless it is navigated at slack high water. Many local people remember the ship HMS Conwy that came to grief on the rocks in 1953 and was subsequently blown up.

Talking of explosives, Morris advocated their use thus: 'all that comes dry between high and low Water Mark of the Skirts of Carreg y Frydain ought to be blown up and carried off; and the Point on the main land opposite to it on the Caernarfonshire Side cut down after the same manner'. This, he continued, 'would widen the Channel, streighten (sic) the Current, and consequently lessen the Velocity, and would prevent Vessels sticking on the Rocks, and oversetting'. Minor adjustments using gunpowder would greatly improve the passage for ships in this part of the country, and he estimated the cost at some two thousand pounds.

It's an easy walk through the woods at Plas Coed Môr down to the water's edge, a couple of hundred metres east of the railway bridge. Even at low water the strong currents can be seen moving swiftly past the rocks. At the waterside, to the right, can be seen the remains of a fish weir built around the back of a small island called Morgan's Island. The main wall is some sixty metres in length and is about 1.5 metres thick. Between the back of the island and the shore is another even smaller island with two short stone walls that dammed this escape route for entrapped fish. Fish swam around the back of the island with the flood, in the opposite direction to the main flood because of an eddy effect, but were then unable to retreat due to the nature of the ebb.

Walk along the shore towards the suspension bridge and a far larger fish weir can still be seen. This is Y Gorad Ddu (or black trap) with stone walls measuring

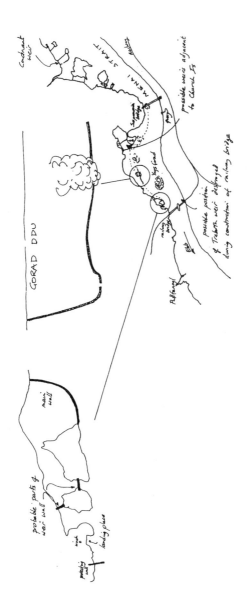

GORAD DDU

Cadnant weir

MENAI STRAIT

possible weirs adjacent to Church S

possible position of Trefarth weir destroyed during construction of railway bridge

railway bridge

Pwllfanogl

main wall

probable parts of weir wall

landing place

127

over two metres high and nearly two metres thick. Once built up with wattled willow, the outer wall reached some one hundred metres across the mouth of a small bay. Curving outwards at the western end, there appears to be the remains of a sluice–gate built into the wall, perhaps allowing the smaller fish to escape. Records tell us of a fishery established at le Borthen (probably Y Borth, Menai Bridge) in 1545, for which the first year's rent was one shilling, subsequently raised to two shillings. It fell into decay as early as 1565. It appears that it was later used for oyster cultivation. These early wattled willow weirs were reputed to have caught fair quantities of immature fish, so that nets were favoured. These seem to have reduced the numbers of small fish being captured.

Near to the fish weir that was first mentioned there is still the remains of an iron winch standing on the foreshore. Offshore, the island of Ynys Gorad Goch lies a hundred metres away. It has been said that this spot, with its steeply shelving beach, was the landing place at one time for the inhabitants of the island. Around the turn of the century there was a bell suspended from a tree that any visitor could ring to summon Huw Madog Jones, the last of three generations of the family that lived on the island until his departure in 1920. His grandfather, William Jones, leased the island from about 1800, while his father, Madog Jones, lived there from his birth in 1820 until his retirement in 1894.

The family relied upon the two fish weirs for their livelihood throughout their residence. These date back to the thirteenth century when herrings – both smoked and fresh – were sent to the monasteries of Amlwch, Caergybi and Penmon. In more recent times thirty thousand herrings were landed at one take in the nineteenth century, while whitebait, herring, sole, mullet, pollack, salmon, as well as other less numerous fish continued to be entrapped up to about the 1960s. Herrings were plentiful during the latter six months of the year and whitebait during the summer season. Occasionally, it seems, other things managed to find their way into the weir, and Old Madog used to relate to visitors how the odd 'nice pig' would find its way in when the swine were being swum across the Strait further up-stream.

There were two weirs on the island, one on the northern and one on the southern side. They were open to the east to allow the ebb tide to flow through the trap and out through grilles in the weir. Fish were swept in and were unable to swim out against the full force of the tide that can reach up to seven knots. The water level dropped by letting the sea water out through the stone walls – the north weir was rebuilt in 1924 so that the solid walls now have gratings that allow the water to flow through but not the fish. The fish are still collected at low water using either lap-nets or a short seine-net for the larger fish. However, the gratings can easily be removed so that nowadays the fish can swim through freely.

As well as the two weirs, there was a Smoke Tower where the herring were cured; the tower remains although it appears not to have been used for very many years. Some have suggested that it was built as a place of worship and later adapted for the curing of fish. Both fresh and cured herring were then taken to the slipway at Porth-y-wrach at nearby Porthaethwy (Menai Bridge), or to the pilot's steps on the Caernarfon side of the Strait near the suspension bridge. At other times it was taken to Pwllfanog. From each of these landing places the catch could be taken by horse and cart to the railway station, either at Porthaethwy or Llanfair Pwllgwyngyll in the latter case. A small boat was kept on the island for this purpose, which was renewed fairly often. Over the period from 1869 to 1914, the fishing record book tell us, new boats were acquired in 1869 (cost £5.0.0), 1890 (£6.7.6d), 1895 (£13.13.6d, old boat sold for £4.10.0d) and 1900 (new boat with sails cost £13.12.0d). Other items of purchase of interest during this period are: nets in 1869 cost thirty shillings, two pairs of oars in 1873 cost 22/6d, wages for three men for ten days in 1879 were £4.4.0, a new sail in 1886 cost seventeen shillings, an iron keel for a boat cost two shillings in 1898 and an anchor cost three shillings in 1914.

In the years preceeding the giving up of the island by Young Madog, visitors journeyed to the island to partake of whitebait teas, this income supplementing the meagre earnings from the fishery. Locals and holiday-makers alike would summon the boat by ringing the bell and be taken over to enjoy the delight of being served the 'Gorad Whitebait Tea'. For one shilling they would eat a basket of fried whitebait, caught in the weir, with brown bread and butter and a pot of tea, before returning by boat to the landing place below Plas Coed Môr woods.

The weirs on the island can easily be seen today from various vantage points. Although ownership remains in private hands – it has remained so since 1888 when it was sold by the Ecclesiastical Commissioner for the church on behalf of its owners, the Bishop of Bangor – the fish weirs, especially the northern one, remain in working order.

I recently had the pleasure of being shown around the island by its current owner. He has spent much time and energy restoring the house to its original character. The smokehouse that stands on Tern Island – they breed there between May and July – has also been restored. The site where the original slate two-seater toilet was once fitted can also be seen.

Much of the northern weir has been rebuilt following the breaching of the weir wall. The wall itself is 5 metres high and 3 metres wide at the base, tapering to the top and runs for a hundred metres or so. There are six openings in the walls that allow the tide to flow through, passing at an estimated six knots on the flood. Above the concrete surface of the wall, a concrete post and rail addition with ballustrading increases the height another 45cm or more. This was covered by water at high tide during my visit. On the other side, the south weir is largely destroyed, but hopefully one day it may be rebuilt. This southern weir was said to have been more effective in capturing fish than the northern one.

Wandering amongst the buildings and in the attractive scented tiny garden, it's easy to imagine visitors munching their fried whitebait in the sun. To the northern side of the house, a veranda and grassy patio give superb views over to Ynys Môn and the Britannia Bridge. The house and the smokehouse have low ceilinged rooms that emanate a sense of the past, a feeling that these rooms with their tiny windows once breathed and lived in a way that we don't see anymore. Who knows, when the work is completed and both weirs are up and in running condition again, then maybe the inherent spirit of this one of the most photographed parts of Anglesey, will revisit it. On my travels around the coast, this was the most evocative, most wonderfully poignant and certainly the most interesting part of the whole journey because it is so tangible. As I said at the beginning, the vast majority of Anglesey's fishing heritage has disappeared. Very few remember the height of the herring season, for instance, yet here the very existence of the weirs, somewhat akin to the Beaumaris weir which survives only in oral history, vibrantly tell the story.

Moving back to Anglesey, it is possible to walk along the muddy beach, except at high-water, to Ynys Tysilio (Church Island) with its little church to St Tysilio and thence onto the Belgian Promenade, to join the road that leads under the suspension bridge and on to the tiny beach at Porth Lladron where the local fishermen used to keep their boats. Further along is the slipway at Porth-y-wrach and then comes the smaller beach of Porth Daniel, next to the timberyard quay which was another useful landing place.

Just beyond Porthaethwy (Menai Bridge) pier is

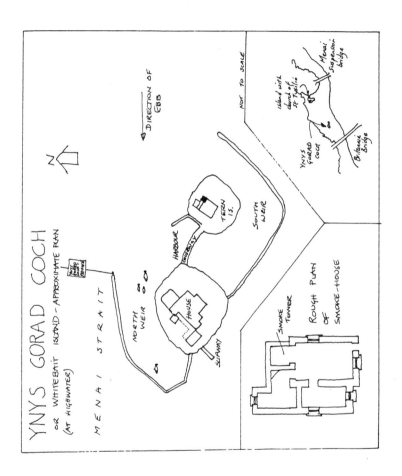

YNYS GORAD COCH
or WHITEBAIT ISLAND – APPROXIMATE PLAN
(AT HIGHWATER)

MENAI STRAIT

N

DIRECTION OF EBB

NORTH WEIR

HOUSE

SLIPWAY

HARBOUR

CAUSEWAY

TERN IS.

SOUTH WEIR

NOT TO SCALE

Island with church of St Tysilio

Menai Suspension bridge

Britannia Bridge

Ynys Gorad Goch

SMOKE TOWER

ROUGH PLAN OF SMOKE-HOUSE

Ynys Faelog where a causeway reaches out from the shore. Here, on the left, is the old boatshed of Matthew Owen who built small open fishing craft for fishermen from Anglesey and Llŷn. The shell of a larger Scottish-style fishing boat has remained on the beach here for many years, which somehow seems to reflect the state of the fisheries hereabout.

Ynys Castell lies 800 metres eastwards, within the mouth of Afon Cadnant, and is joined to Ynys Môn by another causeway. On the westward side of this is another fish weir. The best place, perhaps, to view this is from the new road bridge that carries the main Beaumaris road. Apart from the fact that this fishery dates back to 1649, not much else is known about it except that it was worked into the twentieth century. The remains of the stone walls are very much in evidence, as are a series of poles that are inbedded into the muddy seabed that show the semi-circular shape of the weir. The walls are breached in many places, yet the original opening where the water escaped on the ebb can still be vaguely made out.

Across the Strait another weir called Gorad y Gilt still exists, although this was somewhat altered for oyster breeding at one point. Way in the distance, another extremely large weir is still visible at low water at the mouth of Afon Ogwen, to the east of Bangor.

Between here and Beaumaris, where we started this circumnavigation of Anglesey, one or two boat-houses line the Menai Strait. The Garth ferry once operated between what are now the Gazelle Hotel and Bangor pier, where a very ancient quay is still visible on the lowest of spring tides. Our journey around the coastline has unearthed quite a variety of maritime heritage, vague signs of which still persist in all manner of ways, although much has been lost forever. Walking and travelling these wonderfully varied shores was an enlightening and pleasurable experience, and one that I hope the reader can duplicate in time to come.

Chapter 8

A Total Circumnavigation

Church of St Cwyfan, Porth Cwyfan (church in the bay)

There is of course another way of viewing the Anglesey seashore, and that is by using a boat to circumnavigate the entire coastline. The best option here is to use a small boat to enable it to sail directly onto the beaches, up into the Inland Sea and close to other interesting features. By journeying offshore from the island, the seaborne traveller will sense a certain detachment from the land, like looking onto a scene without being part of it. It's a totally different perception of the rocks, the headlands and the now deserted working coves – apart from the sun worshipping visitors, that is!

The words that I write are not intended to replace the various guides and almanacs for sailors. Assuming that the reader has obtained a suitable craft – my current boat is a 14ft bilge-keeler with berths for two – the other imperative need is a thorough knowledge of the tides. They can be used to increase speed along portions of the coast when timed to flow in the direction of your travel, whilst at other times it is indeed a necessity to arrive at certain points off the coast at slack water. All the guides give this information.

Again commencing at Beaumaris, the ebb tide is taken to Trwyn Du (Penmon Point), past the crumbling mass of Burton's shed where his motor yacht was once kept, past Laird's, past the fish weir where the lifeboat shed once was, past the quay at Penmon with the Priory standing out on the hilltop, and up to the lifeboat house and coastguard cottages at Penmon. Here the narrow channel between the lighthouse and the red beacon leads you out into the open sea, and the feel of the deep beneath the keel is felt for the first time. Although it was noted earlier that the coast westwards from here is inhospitable, there are three or four tiny coves where landings can be managed in suitable wind conditions.

The sweep of Traeth Coch (Red Wharf Bay) is quickly upon you as you pass around the headland below Bwrdd Arthur, and aim for the buoy at the entrance to the narrow channel under Castell-mawr up to the shelter at Porthllongdy. The Ship Inn is conveniently situated for refreshment! Leaving the channel, it's only a short hop round to Benllech. Mind you, this isn't an ideal anchorage, and I have in the past spent an uncomfortable night anchored off with a northeasterly swell producing an unpleasant surf on the beach. When we dragged the anchor in the early hours, I luckily awoke to the sound of the surf which was only yards away. You can imagine the haste with which I started the Seagull outboard so as to get into deeper water!

Heading north, Traeth Bychan can be visited before arriving at Moelfre. Moelfre is a delightful spot with good anchorage in fair weather, and a place with pubs, shops and places to eat, all of which make it a good place to stay overnight. Rounding Ynys Moelfre, Traeth Lligwy lies a mile (1.6km) north, and beyond that is Traeth Dulas. The latter can be entered at or near highwater, but beware the falling tide in case you get stranded.

The coast to the north is again inaccessible from the landward side, yet can be sailed close in so as to admire the rocks. Past Freshwater Bay, named after a nearby spring, the landing place at Trwyn Eilian (Point Lynas) can be seen, and from thence a passage around the lighthouse and into the fairly well sheltered bay of Porth Eilian.

The harbour at Amlwch is easily entered, although it largely dries out at low water. A break either here or at Porth Eilian often allows the sailor to take full advantage of the ebb tide so as to navigate the northern coast of the island. As mentioned before, it is a treacherous coast with strong tides, which will fight you as you sail against them.

Porth Llechog (Bull Bay) lies past Ynys Amlwch (East Mouse) and the chemical works. Shelter from southwesterlies can be found here, although it is exposed from the north and east. Moving eastwards, Porth Wen makes an ideal anchorage, although the holding is poor. The brickworks are well worth a trip ashore to see the remnants of a bygone era. Cemaes, a few miles further east, past Ynys Badrig (Middle Mouse), makes another snug overnight stop, tucked in behind the seemingly solid harbour wall.

Leaving the harbour, the ugly bulk of the nuclear power station is quickly passed, and Cemlyn Bay opens up. The next obstacle after here – having avoided Harry Furlough's rocks that is – is Trwyn y Gader (Carmel Head) where strong tides make a slack water rounding important in a small boat. With local knowledge, Ynysoedd y Moelrhoniaid (the Skerries) can be landed upon with great care. Next along the coastline is Ynys y Fydlyn and then around the next two headlands comes Porth Swtan (Church Bay). From here the coast can easily be followed right into Beddmanarch Bay, perhaps to view the fish weir at the mouth of Afon Alaw. As the Stanley Embankment cannot be passed, one must retrace northwards, avoiding Cerrig y Gwŷr (rocks), and into Holyhead harbour. Moorings can generally be had from the sailing club which is tucked into the southwest corner of the harbour, near the beginning of the breakwater.

The next phase of the passage needs great attention in detail regarding the tides, for rounding the lighthouse at Ynys Lawd (South Stack) can be an unforgetful experience if the wind is against the tide. Extremely nasty overfalls can be experienced (I've been there!) but at slack water there's nothing to worry about in general. Ynys Arw (North Stack) can also be nasty at certain stages of the tide. Arrange to leave Holyhead before high-water to arrive off the Stacks at high-water, and thence obtain the ebb southwards. It's only a few miles onwards to Trearddur Bay which, although touristy, does have some sheltered bays. Alternatively, continue south to Rhoscolyn – taking care to miss the outlying rock of Maen Piscar and the rocks off Rhoscolyn – and anchor in the ideal bay of Borthwen. There is a pub a hundred yards or so up the road from the beach!

Leaving Rhoscolyn, take a detour eastwards, past lovely Silver Bay, to Cymyran. With care, and the right tides, shallow-drafted boats can sail up the channel between Ynys Môn (Anglesey) and Ynys Cybi (Holy Island), possibly up as far as the Rhyd-bont (Fourmile Bridge). Otherwise continue southwards, across Cymyran Bay to Rhosneigr. There's a good anchorage between the off-lying islands and the beach. Facilities can be had here.

South of Rhosneigr are some of Ynys Môn's best beaches, and Porth Trecastell can easily be landed upon. However, there's a car park here which means it can be busy in summer. The church on the island at Porth Gwylan, although not as good a beach, is perhaps a better option for a break in the journey. Around Braich-lwyd lies Aberffraw Bay, and beyond the inaccessible part of the Bodorgan Estate. Landing from the sea onto these beaches might not perhaps be exactly correct, but is certainly worthwhile to enjoy the peace and tranquility of the area.

Across Malltraeth Bay is Ynys Llanddwyn with its perfect anchorage in the Pilot's Cove (Malltraeth itself can be sailed up to, but local knowledge of the waters is necessary). Llanddwyn is an ideal anchorage to wait for the right tides to sail into the Menai Strait. The flood is best in a shallow-draft boat – a deep-draft boat would be unable to sail over Caernarfon Bar at low water – to follow the channel over the bar, past Abermenai Point, and back into the Menai Strait. The main channel keeps to the Caernarfon side, but a detour can easily be made over to the Mermaid Inn at Foel Ferry. The channel then passes Moel-y-don, opposite colourful Felinheli (Port Dinorwig), and then the Strait narrows, passing the Marquis of Anglesey's Plas Newydd, before coming to Pwllfanog. This is a private dock, and it isn't possible to stay.

Ahead lies Stephenson's Britannia Bridge, and beyond the Swellies. Slack water must be found here, otherwise currents of up to seven knots can be encountered as well as whirlpools, as the tide surges through the narrow channel which is littered with rocks. Assuming that you've made a good passage up the Strait on the flood, it might be perfect for a high water slack passing. However, don't forget to have a good glimpse at Ynys Gorad Goch, although a landing is impossible as this is a private island.

The Swellies (Pwll Cerys) end underneath Telford's Suspension Bridge, after which is the town of Porthaethwy with its pier and various moorings. However, with Beaumaris only an hour distant, many will prefer to complete the circumnavigation by proceeding on, past the Gazelle Hotel from where a ferry once ran over to where Bangor pier juts out opposite.

I reckon the total distance around the island by sea to be about eighty miles (130km), allowing for detours into Beddmanarch Bay and the Inland Sea. Large craft can easily sail this in a day, and smaller craft in two. However, so as to fully enjoy the coastline, stopping off on the deserted beaches and viewing the relics of a passed age, four days is the optimum time to allow all this. Whichever way you chose to sail it, and from whatever starting point – boats can be launched from a host of beaches and slipways – and with ideal weather conditions, it is a most pleasant way to circumnavigate the island of Anglesey.